THE GO
RULES
PARENTING

the secrets of
successful parenting

Dorothy Einon

Vermilion
LONDON

C000137842

1 3 5 7 9 10 8 6 4 2

Text © Dorothy Einon 2002

First published in the United Kingdom in 2002 by Vermilion
an imprint of Ebury Press
Random House
20 Vauxhall Bridge Road · London SW1V 2SA

Random House Australia (Pty) Limited
20 Alfred Street · Milsons Point · Sydney · New South Wales 2061 · Australia

Random House New Zealand Limited
18 Poland Road · Glenfield · Auckland 10 · New Zealand

Random House South Africa (Pty) Limited
Endulini · 5A Jubilee Road · Parktown 2193 · South Africa

Papers used by Vermilion are natural, recyclable products made from
wood grown in sustainable forests

A CIP catalogue record for this book is available from the British Library

ISBN 0 09 188285 0

Designed by Lovelock & Co.

Printed and bound in Great Britain by Mackays of Chatham plc · Chatham · Kent

CONTENTS

Introduction   4

The fundamental rules   7

Practicalities   17

The Rules of Love   71

The Nature of Children   95

Staying in Control   121

How to Treat Children   139

Technique   191

Introduction

This is a book of loving rules and principles that allow parents to nurture and encourage their children while at the same time setting clear boundaries for them. The first aim of the book is to show parents how best to set an agenda for children that ensures the formation of warm affectionate relationships and encourages children to develop high self-esteem, self-confidence and self-discipline. The second aim is to show parents how they can best provide the sort of safe and secure background that gives each child the confidence to go out and explore the world.

The central ethos of the book is that clear and consistent rules make children feel secure. Bear in mind, that if small children are allowed to choose they will usually wear the same clothes, eat the same food and watch the same video every time and that this 'stick in the mud' attitude serves an important purpose: when the basics are predictable the child's mind is freed to learn and discover.

Because a child has a very limited ability to think about more than one thing at a time, a home life without clear rules is a home life filled with constant worry, stress and distraction and the child is too busy checking that he has 'got it right' and is 'pleasing those who need to be pleased' to get on with the real business of learning. Faced with such insecurity he finds it hard to explore new ideas. For such children there is change enough in their lives without seeking pastures new! On the other hand, if the rules of 'day to day living' are so clear to the child that they have become completely automatic, he does not have to think about the rules,

stress drops away and he is free to explore new ideas. Put another way if his 'frustration quota' is tied up with working out what to do, he does not have the 'calm' to tackle anything which is inherently difficult.

As a general principle the rules you will find here are more concerned with avoiding the necessity of constantly disciplining children, than showing parents which disciplinary techniques work – although the rules of discipline are also included. There is, after all, no such thing as a technique that works every time, any more than there are perfectly behaved parents or perfectly behaved children. It is also in the nature of children to put up a spirited opposition from time to time. No child can be good all the time. Nor should anyone expect them to be.

The Golden Rules are based on well-established learning principles:
- that learning (and teaching) can occur without awareness,
- that anticipation and expectation are powerful controlling forces for behaviour,
- that children do what they are rewarded for doing,
- and that feeling good about themselves, and what they do makes learning easier. And it also instills confidence in them.

I have taken as a given that all parents reading this book want to raise a happy and loving child who can form relationships and function in the world and in society with a reasonable amount of success. Beyond this I suggest that you spend some time thinking about the things that really matter to them. The rules should then show you how to guide your children in the direction they want to go.

Children need clear and consistent limits – but quite where each family draws the limit is up to them. These rules show you how to set limits. They do not say what those limits should be. Some families may wish to ensure a quiet time each night after the children are in bed. Others may be perfectly happy to have the children around until they themselves go to bed. Some may feel that swearing is unimportant, others may hold a very different view. These are personal matters which each family must decide for themselves.

At the beginning of the book you will find the fundamental rules or wisdoms which underpin all the rules that follow. These are followed by a set of practical rules and principles, the rules governing love and the nature of children and these are followed by sections on staying in control, how to treat children and a final section on specific techniques, and problem solving.

Parents should lead by example because small children are more influenced by your actions than your words. The younger your child, the more this is the case. The message must be clear in your actions and in your body language if you want the child to comply. Not just in what you say.

Finally, small children rarely initiate change. If parents want things to be different they must initiate those changes. Which is why many of these rules concern what parents do, rather more than what children do. Be fair; be consistent; be constructive; be resilient; be positive and polite and sort issues out – and if you don't yet do these things you can learn alongside your child.

THE FUNDAMENTAL
RULES

1 From the very start there have to be consistent rules. Those rules should socialize children and lead them to believe:

- ■ I'm loved without question.
- ■ I can if I try.
- ■ I'm worth it.
- ■ It matters what I do and how I behave towards myself and other people.

Rules are a child's security blanket. They let the child know where they stand and how they should behave. The world is a frightening place if you are small, dependent and do not know how to control what will happen to you. Bear in mind that it is the things that are unpredictable and out of our control that produce most stress.

The rules that work best are those that have become completely ingrained habits. If we have to think about whether we should or should not, we are almost certainly part way to breaking the rule. An irregular bedtime is a pathway to insomnia, irregular eating habits a pathway to snacking and

  The Golden Rules of Parenting

binge eating; and inconsistent expectations of how children ought to behave, and inconsistent responses to them when they misbehave (or get it right) make children difficult, disruptive and insecure. Start as you mean to go on and set those things that matter to your family in stone.

Never lose sight of the bigger picture. The long-term aim of all parents is to enable children to live and survive outside the family: in effect to be their own parent. Rules are about more than getting children to do what they are told. Again they should lead children to believe:

- I'm loved without question by my family.
- I can do it if I try and my efforts will be valued.
- I'm worth it (I have high self-esteem).
- I should expect and give fair treatment.

There is no such thing as a perfect child, a perfect family or a perfect parent. All we can do is our best, and if we fall off our pedestals now and again, that's life. We just have to find the ladder we can climb up again. Both parents and children should know this.

2 Children have a fundamental right to their parents' unquestioning love, the provision of a balanced diet, warmth and protection from harm.

Everything else is an extra that needs to be earned.

Children should never have to earn your love, but they do need to earn your indulgence. They should not have to earn their daily bread, but there is absolutely no reason why a badly behaved child should think that chocolate pudding is his by right.

What you give beyond the basic provision you give because he has shown he is worth it.

If YOU want to dress him in expensive T-shirts and the very latest in trainers it's your money and your problem, but if HE wants you to indulge his desire for such things, he has to give something in return.

That something is reasonable behaviour, active family membership and adherence to family rules and values.

3 Parents do not have a fundamental right to their children's love and respect. They earn that right.

Babies come into the world with a suitcase of love which they scatter willy-nilly upon those around them. It is what babies do.

But that does not mean parents have a right to their children's love.

- A child has every right to withdraw his love when parents mistreat him.
- A child does not have to give love to an abusive parent.
- A child does not have to love a parent who could provide for him but chooses not to do so, or who takes what is due to the child for him/herself.

The contract parents make when they undertake to raise children is to love them come hell or high water. However badly behaved a child is, he does not lose the right to his parents' love.

Parents earn the right to their children's love and respect by:

- Loving their children and showing that love.
- Making good provision for their family and ensuring a safe and secure environment.
- Providing a transparent set of rules for children to live by.
- Assuming children are capable of living by those rules and expecting that they will.
- Setting children a good example. If a child is taught that certain values are important, a parent who consistently fails to adhere to those values ultimately loses the child's respect.
- The respect parents show to themselves. It is always harder to love and respect those who do not love and respect themselves.

4 Rewards work better than punishments; praise works better than criticism.

The positive

If an action leads to a desirable end, children repeat the action. They also repeat actions that lead to the removal of something undesirable. Getting it right gets us what we want, but more than that, it gives us a 'Hey I did that' effect that raises our spirits and makes us feel good about ourselves.

Add the praise of someone who means something to us and there is a nice warm afterglow. When we feel good we find it easier to achieve, so getting it right once activates the built-in ratchet that lifts the child towards more success.

The negative

Whether it's a slap to the hand or to the ego, the natural response to being hurt is to feel angry and want to fight back. We don't feel good about ourselves, so achievement is that bit harder.

  The Golden Rules of Parenting

Add the criticism of someone we care about and it feels much worse. Because we find it harder to achieve when we feel badly about ourselves, criticism makes it harder to succeed.

Because small children have short memories and are so easily distracted, these ups and downs are fleeting. Whether it's a smile of pleasure or a petulant lip it's all soon forgotten. As children grow up, their moods persist for longer and the colour of that mood has more far-reaching effects. Once changed, the mood persists, affecting not only what has gone before but also what follows.

- Punishment stops one behaviour in its tracks, but also puts a negative gloss on what follows.
- Praise draws out the first behaviour and puts a happy gloss on what follows.

In other words, the older children are, the more successful are reward and praise in controlling their behaviour, and the less successful are punishment and criticism.

PRACTICALITIES

5 Consider your strategies.

There are two basic strategies for the smooth running of all families:

- Stop rewarding bad behaviour by giving it attention and making it important.
- Start rewarding good behaviour.

The carrot works better than the stick.
A child should always have more attention paid to his good behaviour than he does to his bad behaviour. Bear in mind that what a small child wants most in the whole world is to be the pivot of the family, the special one, the one who engages your thoughts more than any other – the absolute centre of your attention.

- If he finds it easier to do this by being naughty, he will be naughty.
- If he finds it easier to do this by being good, he will be good.

  The Golden Rules of Parenting

It is your choice.

If you realise that you are rewarding bad behaviour don't panic. You can change things but it's tough and it needs YOU to act with complete consistency.

- When you start with a blank slate and teach one strategy, there is just the learning to do.
- When you try to change the unacceptable ways your child behaves to gain attention, such as being disruptive or squabbling with his sibling, you have to first break what are often engrained habits on both sides before you can set up more acceptable attention giving and seeking strategies.

The onus is on you to change because:

- While it is working for the child, he has no reason to change.
- It is not working for you, so changes have to be made.
- You have more foresight and know that reducing family upset is ultimately more rewarding for everyone.

6 Making reasonable demands on children helps them to become good and considerate people.

When parents complain about their children's behaviour they are usually assuming that their children should be indebted to them: that in one respect or another it's mostly give on the parents' side and mostly take on the children's. There is no point in blaming children for this state of affairs. It is human nature for a child to take advantage when allowed. If you want consideration from children (as from anyone else), you must ask for it. If it is lacking you should initiate change that will reinstate it. Selflessness is not a prerequisite to good parenting: on the contrary, selflessness in one party tends to encourage selfishness in another. Making reasonable demands on children helps them to become good and considerate people.

Ways in which children are often indebted to parents

- Family food is often the children's favourite.
- Outings tend to be to places the children choose.
- The TV is switched to the channel they want to watch.

The Golden Rules of Parenting

- Childen demand clothes and toys parents cannot afford.
- The living room is scattered with dirty cups and plates, towels need to be retrieved from the bedrooms, the table has not been cleared, and you have to collect the dirty washing from the floor.
- You get no help in the house; you shop, cook, clean, and find and wash their gym kits while they watch TV.

But why should they change? The only thing that stops us being entirely selfish is that our actions have consequences, and that some paths ultimately provide more guilt than pleasure. In later years, your child's partner may tell him: 'Your mother may have enjoyed waiting on you, but I don't' while your therapist would probably ask you: 'Why do you need to do it all yourself?'

There is no reason. Families in the past shared chores. Only slaves and servants did it all. So cast aside the guilt and martyrdom and redress the balance. Start expecting them to think about family needs, not just themselves. Expect help. Make their benefits contingent on their good and helpful behaviour. Start asking, what's in it for ME?

7 Children crave their parents' attention.

Go back 1,500 generations to the days when humans lived as semi-nomadic hunter-gatherers. There were no safe toys or childproofed rooms; in order to survive, small children had to keep reminding busy parents of their existence. Those that did not could swallow poisonous fruits, wander off or get left behind. We are the same people they were, and our children are like theirs. Thinking of how our ancestors lived helps us to understand why children are programmed to prefer any form of attention to being ignored. Of course they prefer a smile and some words of praise, but if all else fails shouting or even smacking are better than nothing. While parents shout they also check; when they ignore they do not.

Attention-seeking is a basic survival mechanism. The child has a need that is met by ANY behaviour that reliably gains his caregiver's attention. If we readily give attention to his bad behaviour, he is more likely to be naughty when he feels needy.

This does not mean he is intentionally or deliberately naughty. He is probably quite unaware of what he is doing, just as we are quite unaware that we are encouraging bad behaviour by giving it immediate and consistent attention.

Children simply learn to repeat those behaviours that most reliably get them what they need. Nature tells children to maintain their parents' attention at all times because parents are the source of food, shelter and protection.

8 Children do what we reward them for doing.

If a certain behaviour consistently leads to a desired result it will be repeated. Psychologists call this operant conditioning. It's a simple and basic form of learning that can occur without us necessarily realizing that anything is happening. Psychologists would say it takes place at a preconscious level, which is to say, we could in principle work out what is going on, but in practice rarely bother to do so.

* Caregivers can teach children things they are not aware of teaching them.
* Children can learn things that they are not aware they have learned.
* Research tells us that it is the most reliable association between an action and a reward that is 'conditioned'.

Staying in control of our children means we sometimes have to step back and examine what is happening.

- We must become aware that consistently rewarding a behaviour by giving it our undivided attention conditions it.
- This increases the likelihood that the behaviour will be repeated next time the child is in need of attention.
- If you always show your appreciation of his good behaviour, he learns a foolproof way of getting your approval. He is good.
- If you often ignore him when he is good, but always pay attention when he is naughty, he learns that the most reliable way to get your attention is to be naughty.

Parents rarely realize they are teaching children to be naughty, and certainly do not intend to do so. Nor do children realize why they are being naughty. It is just something that happens when rewards reliably follow certain behaviours.

9 Do not give attention to bad behaviour.

The early weekday morning is always a flash point. Parents need time to themselves while they get shaved or put on their make-up. Who doesn't like to contemplate the day as they drink their morning tea? From our point of view this is the worst possible time for the boys to squabble over which of them has the bowl with the red rim, or for the three-year-old to have a tantrum because the heel of her sock isn't on the heel of her foot.

They create, and we wade in:

Be quiet . . .

Oh for heaven's sake . . .

Can't we just have one morning without you lot . . .

Our attention is stolen from our own needs and we are once more the fully functioning parent.

By rewarding badly behaved children with our undivided attention, we make it more likely that next time they feel left out they will behave this way again, though not necessarily intentionally or deliberately. The three-year-old is not deliberately putting her sock on heel uppermost, or pretending it matters when it does not. She is almost certainly quite unaware of why she is behaving badly, just as we are quite unaware that when we turn from our own concerns to give her our full attention, we are rewarding bad behaviour.

The point to remember is that children need attention. Given a choice, they would take our smiling, loving attention. But if the choice is between being totally ignored and having our undivided bad temper, they take the bad temper every time. If you have ever picked a quarrel or 'had a headache' because you think you are being taken for granted by your partner, you may sympathize.

10 Children will keep on pestering us if we allow them to.

If he knows he will get his own way in the end, why should a child stop pestering until you give in? If you say no five times then give in, it is worth him pushing his case. If after saying no you sometimes change your mind if he nags enough, he pesters.

* Say exactly what you mean and mean exactly what you say.
* Say it once.
* If you say you will act, act.
* If you say no, mean it.
* Ignore his prevarication.

Don't get into arguments, state the facts:

> *You cannot have a biscuit before lunch. That's the rule.*
> *We only buy sweets at the corner shop on sweetie day.*

If he persists, act. Get down to his level. Look him in the eye:

> *I expect you to stop that NOW.*

If he does:

> *Thank you, Tom. I really appreciate that.*

  The Golden Rules of Parenting

Praise him if he does not pester when he might:

It's hard when you see all those sweets. Thank you for not
pestering me today.

If he does not stop, go straight to the 'one two three':

I am going to count to three, and if you have not stopped
pestering you will go straight to your room . . . one, two, three . . .

If he does stop:

Thank you for stopping.

And if he does not:

Go to your room; come down when you are ready to say sorry.

Do not threaten more than you will carry through. You are NOT
going to ban sweets for ever or leave him in the car while you
finish shopping; so don't say you will. Be prepared to leave the
shop without returning (if this punishes him), or to go out of
the shop and sit in the car until he is willing to behave. Return
to complete the shopping; be wary of giving him a way of
avoiding shopping with you in future!

11 You have to set limits for children.

How is a child to know what he can and cannot do unless you let him know? How can he understand rules if the rules depend on your mood? To feel secure, children must know exactly where they stand, which means they need clear, concise and consistent limits.

Where you set those limits depends on the needs and expectations of your family. It does not matter if you are stricter or more indulgent than the other parents in your street, providing you are consistent. You can be firm about some things, more indulgent about others. It's a family choice. Where precisely you set your limits is unimportant, providing everyone understands what the rules are, they are consistently applied and do not change from day to day.

In this house we do not allow people to swear at each other.
On weekdays bedtime is 8.30. That is the rule, you have school tomorrow. I am not prepared to discuss this any further.

If you allow a few exceptions make this clear:

> *If you get your pyjamas on and clear up your toys, you can stay*
> *up to watch the dinosaur programme. It's a special treat, mind.*
> *As a special treat we will cuddle up and eat our biscuits and drink*
> *our drinks in front of the TV.*

If rules change, let them know:

> *You are now old enough to decide when you go to bed, but if I need*
> *to call you every morning we go back to 10 p.m. in the week.*
> *You are old enough to make your own decisions about your*
> *homework, but if you want help from your father or me you*
> *need to put in effort first.*

As night follows day they will push up against any limits that you set. This is natural. Children are not born knowing right from wrong. They learn by testing the rules we set to find exactly where the boundary lies and where (or if) it varies in different conditions. If you constantly give way, children do not have the security of a firm boundary. This makes learning more difficult and they need to test and retest in order to try and establish the rules. They constantly push the limits and in doing so learn that if they push hard enough you reward them by backing down.

12 You must make the family rules clear.

Everything is black and white for a small child; this means they are happiest if the rules are set out clearly and concisely.

> *In this house we do not hit each other, that is the rule.*
> *George, James can say what happens to things that belong to him, that is the rule.*
> *We do not take things that do not belong to us.*
> *Hurting people is wrong.*

- Children need to know what happens if they keep rules (praise, rewards) and what happens if rules are broken (loss of privileges, punishments).
- Some families like to write the rules out for the children and pin them up. It can work very well. (Even if they can't read, you can point to the rule and read it out following the words with your finger.)
- Some families make contracts that both parties sign. Consider getting older children to sign a 'behavioural agreement', accepting the rules, the consequences of living

by them (rewards) and the consequences of breaking them (losing rewards, punishments).

- Remember that many of the trappings of modern life (a mobile phone, TV in the bedroom) are not the child's by right; he should understand that he earns these things by his good behaviour and can lose them.
- Rewarding the good usually works better than punishing the bad.

Do not threaten to act on those rules:

If I see you two hitting each other again, you'll go to your room.

Act. If 'do not hit' is a rule, and time-out in his room the punishment, the child should be on his way to his room before you make this threat.

Do not give extra chances:

If you do that again, I'll . . .

I'm not going to tell you again . . .

If children are given extra chances the rule becomes 'I can do it three times before Mum stops me'.

Act every time; firmly, precisely and within the letter of the law.

13 Hone your tactics.

There are eight basic tactics for getting children to do what you want.

1   Give attention to good behaviour and avoid giving attention to bad behaviour.
2   Praise, compliment and reward your child for effort, success and good behaviour, for being helpful, generous or kind, and for abiding by the family rules.
3   Turn things that need to be done (but everyone hates doing) into a game, such as picking up the toys before the music stops, seeing who can find the most pairs in the odd sock pile, or making a silly-rhyme shopping list for the supermarket (Where is the dead bread? Where are Clare's pears?).

4   Letting the child reap the natural consequence of his
    behaviour teaches him to take responsibility for his actions.
    If he refuses to wear his gloves, his hands get cold.
    (Obviously we sometimes have to intervene here, but do
    not jump in too quickly. If it's just cold hands, let it
    happen. If there is a potential for frostbite, clearly we need
    to insist.)

5   Once a child is old enough to think logically (at about the
    age of seven), letting him reap the logical consequences of
    his behaviour teaches him to take responsibility for his
    actions. If he does not remember to take his lunch to school
    he goes hungry. If he leaves the football out the front
    someone will take it. Clearly we have a responsibility to
    stop the child from putting himself in danger; we don't
    have a responsibility to replace the football.

6   Encourage good behaviour by using charts and contracts.

7   Expect payment (in terms of good behaviour) for special
    treats, and give rewards for good behaviour which is
    beyond the call of duty.

8   Expect obedience, but acknowledge it with a thank you
    when it occurs.

14 The easiest (and nicest) way to control children is to reward their good behaviour.

Rewards give pleasure and satisfaction so children will try to maximize the number they receive. Used effectively, the giving and withholding of rewards is the easiest and most reliable way to shape children's behaviour. But rewards have to be given consistently.

- The most important reward for a small child is their caregiver's attention, affection and love. A soft rain of smiles and encouragement should reward good behaviour.
- While we set the behavioural goals and agenda, we must also provide the rewards.
- Being good is not its own reward until children know how to be good. We have to teach them.
- Succeeding is a reward in itself, and success lures children along the approved path. As they grow up, children set their own goals, and achieving those goals acts as their reward.

  The Golden Rules of Parenting

When children behave well they need:

- A glance or smile.
- A few words of approval: 'Good', 'Well done', 'I'm really pleased'.
- Encouragement: 'That's right', 'You can do it'.
- The boosting of esteem and a sense of achievement: 'You really did that so well', 'What a star'.

When they are not being good, they should get none of these things. Avert your eyes, look away, remove the child from your sight.

Reward works best if you keep in mind Rule 2. Nothing but love and basic survival comes for free.

Rewards fall into three groups:

- **Interim rewards**. Immediate rewards which serve to lure the child forward.
- **Daily rewards** which are promised as a result of good behaviour and collected that day or the next.
- **Weekly rewards** that are worked towards by gaining points for good behaviour all week.

15 Try token economies and star charts – they really do work.

Token economies were developed to control the behaviour of mentally handicapped patients in large hospitals. They worked so well that those who developed the technique suggested parents should try them – they did, and found that they worked.

The basic idea is that the child is immediately given a small token reward for good behaviour. The token – points, or stars on a chart – can later be cashed in for something he wants. Ten points could buy his choice of dinner, 50 points a trip to the cinema.

Star charts work exceptionally well to reward effort and point children in the right direction, especially when the child does not know how to start to take control. For example, a child may not know how to control his temper. But by rewarding him for each half-hour he manages to go without losing his temper (later an hour, then two), you reward whatever it is the child does when he keeps anger under control. You do not need to know how he does this, and nor does he; all he has to do is keep doing whatever it is he was doing when he gained the star. It sounds like mumbo-jumbo but it is not. Bear in mind that rewards work at a preconscious level. Children do not need to be aware of why they were rewarded for a reward to be effective. Star charts have been used effectively to reduce the incidence of disruption, tantrums, soiling and bed-wetting, and to encourage anger management and concentration.

How star charts work

For day 1–3: one star for every five minutes he stays in bed in the morning.

For days 4–6: one star for every ten minutes he stays in bed in the morning.

For days 7–9: one star for every half-hour he stays in bed in the morning.

Exchange stars for treats.

How points systems work

One point for good behaviour.

Two points for negotiating a more difficult task.

Three points for lending his best toys to his friends.

Exchange points for treats.

16 Give your child a soft rain of little rewards – and save up for something bigger.

Interim rewards

These serve to lure children along the right path and should be given like a gentle rain.

- Attention: looking, nodding, glancing up, blowing a kiss.
- Encouragement: words of encouragement and praise. Smiles, hugs, pats, cuddles and kisses, pride shown, praise given.
- Engagement: shared laughter and conversation. Getting down to the child's level, looking him in the eye and saying, 'You're great!' Getting involved. Doing things together. Helping with a difficult bit.
- Forgiveness: when he is sorry.
- Apology: when you are wrong.

Withdrawing interim rewards

- Looking away.
- Going out of the room.
- Putting on an emotionless face.

Small daily rewards

A cashing-in of stars or points – or because he has been good and you feel like rewarding him.

- A special meal, snack or dessert.
- Watching a TV programme, or a video.
- Extra time on the computer, the internet or a games console.
- An extra story at bedtime.
- Staying up late, or going to the park.
- Digging for worms, or a messy game.
- A special and exclusive time with one parent.

Weekly rewards, and special treats to aim for

- Play a family game or go on an outing of their choosing.
- Rent a video, have a friend to tea.
- Buy a new book, video, toy or game.
- Camp in the garden.
- Go swimming or on a bike ride.

Withdrawing daily or weekly rewards

When he has been naughty or particularly badly behaved:

- No snacks or dessert today.
- No bedtime story. No special time.
- Delaying or losing a promised reward.

17 Living together is about making contracts: it sometimes helps to formalize them.

Charts and point systems work well in the short term, but contracts work better for behaviour which needs to be controlled over a longer period, or when the issue arises infrequently.

A contract is very simple. Both parties get together and agree:

- What needs to be done.
- What the consequences are for doing it.
- Whether there are exceptions.

So for example the contract might be:

Tom agrees to tidy his room every Saturday. In exchange Mum agrees to give Tom extra pocket money (specify how much) or to allow him to stay up until 9.30 to watch TV. Tom to make this choice. For the purpose of this contract, tidying includes:

- Putting toys and clothes away.
- Doing this neatly and putting things in the proper place.
- Picking things up off the floor.
- Putting all rubbish in the bin.
- Vacuuming.

Then you both sign the contract and put it in the contract book. If the child keeps to the contract, he gets the contracted reward. If he does not keep to the contract, he gets nothing.

18 Finding and using punishment effectively is extremely difficult. It's not about vindictiveness; it's about helping him to change.

The aim of punishment is:

- To bring unwanted behaviour to a halt immediately.
- To indicate to the child that he has overstepped the mark.
- To help direct him towards the right path.

It's *not* about vindictiveness; it's about helping him to change and making our limits and boundaries absolutely clear to him.

Punishment should be fair and consistent. Your first thought should be: 'How best can I change him?' It should *never, ever* be: 'What's the appropriate amount of hurt, or how can my punishment fit this crime?'

Punishment should also be relatively rare. If you are constantly punishing the child for a certain behaviour, it is clearly not having any effect and you need to examine your tactics. It is always better to encourage and control good behaviour and steer children towards an alternative and acceptable action rather than punish them AFTER they have done the wrong thing.

When children overstep the mark, let them know quickly and firmly:

- By describing what they have done.
- By telling them it is unacceptable – and why.
- By imposing a consequence.
- By expecting a proper apology.
- By forgiving and forgetting once the situation is rectified.

A child should always know why he is being punished. He may be surprised at being caught out, but once he understands that his action was wrong, he should never be surprised at the consequence of that action.

If the child does not know he has overstepped the mark you have a basic problem in setting your limits. YOU need to put this right.

19 If a behaviour needs stopping in its tracks try 'three counts and you are out'.

'Three counts and you are out' is a useful technique when you need to put a stop to certain behaviours. It is not the way to teach responsibility, but it can be very effective:

- When your child is in the process of doing something wrong.
- When he is unwilling to take no for an answer.
- When you need to cut short an argument.
- When you need immediate obedience.

Stay calm. Do not shout or show emotion. Make eye contact if possible and tell the child what he must do.

Sarah give that pen back now.
Jamie pick up that coat now.
Sam please put the game away now.

  The Golden Rules of Parenting

If he does not respond, hold his gaze, pause for a (silent) count of two and say, 'That's one.'

Nothing more, do not threaten or repeat the instruction. Stay calm and controlled. Stand facing him, but do not approach, put on a serious expression, hold his gaze, and if he does not do as he was asked after a few seconds, say, 'That's two.'

No threats, no please, no requests, just those two little words. Wait a couple of seconds, and if he has still done nothing say, 'That's three; go to time-out.'

Pick up a young child and put him outside the door. For an older child point to the door. If he does nothing, say, 'Time-out starts when you are in your room. Unless you go immediately, you will lose privileges.'

Giving instructions once and only once and following up with a clear action ends the incident quickly, curtails argument, and gives you authority.

20 If children are misbehaving and it does not affect you directly, your best tactic may be to ignore them.

Mum he's taken my pen.
She won't give me my book.
But he took mine first.
Says who?

There are times when you can't win: when you don't know who started it, and you are pretty sure that once you have sorted this one out, they will find something else to bicker about. These are the times when the only thing to do is leave them to it. Go into another room, make yourself a cup of tea and read the paper. Once settled, you can always ask them in a perfectly matter-of-fact way, 'Do either of you want a drink?' The message you should give them is: 'As far as I'm concerned, nothing is happening here.'

If the dispute cranks up a notch, just describe what you see, tell them you have confidence they can sort it out, and walk away.

The Golden Rules of Parenting

So George has a pen that Jane wants, Jane has a book that George wants – well, it's a difficult one, but I'm sure you two can sort it out.

When siblings squabble, they are learning how to stand their ground and sort out their own problems – something that is better and more easily learned in the home without interference. All you do by wading in too quickly is delay the learning process. You also teach them that a good squabble is a surefire way of getting your attention.

The sooner they start to learn this skill, the better. If you intervene each time they squabble, you'll just create a full-time job for yourself and put off any attempt by them to sort things out for themselves.

21 Time-out is what the books always tell you to do: because it works!
It teaches little ones that naughty behaviour has consequences and shows them that by changing back to good behaviour they get more attention.

Time-out is a technique that is best used for behaviours which are wrong – such as spitting, hitting, answering back – rather than irresponsible behaviour. It must be used consistently so that the child knows that the immediate consequence of his action is:

- Time-out from your attention.
- Time-out from having fun.
- Time-out from being with others.
- Time-out from rewards.

Time-out is not a severe punishment that acts as a one-off and all-time cure. It is a gradual process that gives the child four messages:

The Golden Rules of Parenting

1 Your behaviour is unacceptable.

2 Your behaviour will not be tolerated.

3 Your behaviour must change.

4 You will not get away with it.

Time-out for toddlers and under-fives

Either pick up the child and put him outside the door, or stand up, put on a blank expression and walk away. If he follows, look away. When this is not possible, pick him up, hold him very tight and either look away or look him in the eye with a completely expressionless stare.

Let him make contact again when he is good and ready. If he is still misbehaving, remove him again. If he has calmed down, say: 'I'm glad you have decided to turn on your good behaviour, because we want you back with us.' He can walk right back into the room as soon as he goes out, as long as he is his old good self when he returns. He is learning that bad means separation from pleasure, while good means being back together.

22 You may need to change the time-out tactics for older children.

1 Select a time-out room. His bedroom, the passageway, the bathroom. The timeout room does not have to be bare. This is not solitary confinement; it's time-out from what he had chosen to do. Let him play or read in the room by all means. But take the lead from the computer and unplug the TV.

2 Either tell the child to go to his room and return when he is ready to say he is sorry and take responsibility for his own good behaviour (good for a one-off bad behaviour).

3 Or impose a period of time-out (especially if the child has ignored warnings and refused to do as he is asked). Set this with a timer – it starts when he stops shouting or otherwise creating a fuss. A good rule of thumb is one minute per year of age. If he starts ranting and raving, time-out starts all over again once he is quiet.

4 Do not interact during time-out under any circumstances. If he needs a wee he can wait a few minutes. If he keeps making a fuss simply say, 'I will start the timer when you start to behave' and leave.

 The Golden Rules of Parenting

5 The child must stay in the room. If he comes out, the clock restarts. If he keeps on coming out of the room, put a bolt on the outside of the door and lock him in. Do not suggest this is jail. If he is prepared to stay in his room and take his punishment, you do not use the lock. If he comes out and you have to return him, you then slip the bolt. Most children accept their punishment first time once they know the lock is present.

6 If he wrecks his room, ignore him. Say nothing and leave the room exactly as it is until the incident is well and truly over. You can discuss his responsibility for tidying up later in the day. Obviously you will need to deal with broken glass and other dangers, but clearing up the mess is his responsibility. Do not replace toys he has broken or books he has ripped.

7 When it's over, it's over. There is nothing to discuss.

If you want to teach the child responsibility, you need to use something with more far-reaching consequences, such as letting the child take the logical consequence of his action.

23 Chores, community service and loss of privileges punish older children.

The five-minute work chore

The child carries out a quick chore that would not normally be part of his responsibility. Obviously, the task you set needs to be appropriate for the age of the child (a five-year-old could not clean the bath, but he could empty the waste-paper baskets). If the child refuses, he loses privileges.

- Picking up rubbish from the front garden.
- Emptying the waste paper baskets.
- Taking the rubbish out to the bin.
- Cleaning the toilet.
- Cleaning the bath.

Community service

This is a punishment for a more serious offence, and is similar to the five-minute work chore – but the chore is carried out more than once. For example, the child might have to clean the toilet for the next four days. Once community service is set, it must be carried out to the letter, so do not impose it unless you are sure you

The Golden Rules of Parenting

can carry it through. Make the alternative punishment clear from the start. If he fails to do the task say 'I see you have decided to pay the fine instead.' Having already agreed it would be 50p for every task not completed, it will be taken off his pocket money at the rate of 50p per week. This way you have a sanction up your sleeve.

Losing privileges

The bottom line is that all children are entitled to love and the basic requirements for life – and that everything else is an extra that must be earned, which means it can also be lost. For example, you could:

- Take away the lead from the computer so he cannot use it for the rest of the day.
- Confiscate his mobile phone until tomorrow.
- Only put sandwiches in his lunch box without the extra treats.

Don't threaten to do what you are not prepared to (or cannot) carry through, and do not go back on what you say. It is best to keep the punishment confined to that day, so you can start each day afresh with a clean slate. Obviously as children grow up it may be necessary to alter this – and remove privileges for longer periods.

24 Grounding is a poor way of imposing control unless you are prepared to have a bad-tempered, bored child around the house for an extended period. Your ultimate sanction should be a return to his basic rights: and the need for him to earn his privileges.

The problem with grounding is that, unlike time-out, children do not have to 'do the right thing' in order to be welcomed back into the fold. They simply have to wait out their time, getting grumpy and self-righteous. Because they're at home, it is the parents who take the full force of this. Grounding fails because the punishment imposed is usually too long to be carried out in full. You should remember that:

- Having a bad-tempered and truculent teenager around nonstop is as much of a punishment to you as it is to him.
- A week is plenty of time to get self-righteous.
- Once you've grounded him for a week you have pretty much run out of options. What next? Ground him for a month?

- It is better to respond to bad behaviour with something quick and short-lived.

Remember, children have a basic right to our love and protection and a subsistence diet but everything else must be earned. If things are bad enough to consider grounding him for long periods, you need to revert to this rule. Remind him that if he wants Coke and hamburgers, pocket money and treats, and a lift around to his friend's, he has to earn those privileges by good and cooperative behaviour. Tell him:

You can cooperate, or we revert to basics. Growing up in a wealthy country has led you to believe that certain things are yours by right. They are not. We pay for your privileges and we are not prepared to keep on doing so unless and until you give something in return.

Be careful, however, that you do not threaten what you cannot, or are not prepared to carry out. Sit down with the child and list his privileges, and ask him what he thinks he should do to pay for them. What would he expect in your position? Then come to an agreement on what he needs to do to maintain his present lifestyle.

25 If you want them to become responsible you have to let them take the consequences.

Letting the child reap the consequences of his behaviour teaches him to take responsibility for his actions. If he refuses to wear his gloves, his hands get cold. If he leaves his book on the lawn, it gets wet. If we soften the blow (by giving him our gloves), we fail to teach.

- As long as we are prepared to take responsibility, our children will let us do so.
- Let the child take full responsibility for his actions – don't run after him. If he does not remember to take his lunch to school, he goes hungry. If he leaves his football in the garden, someone will take it. If we constantly remind him, he does not take full responsibility. If we replace what he loses or spoils, how will he learn responsibility?

The Golden Rules of Parenting

- If a child is very forgetful you may find it helps if you teach him to ask himself 'Have I got everything?' before he leaves the house, or to write a check list for the bedroom wall which he consults before leaving for school.
- Clearly you cannot leave a child to face the dangerous consequences of his actions.
- Consider whether he should make a contribution towards the careless damage he has caused to other people's property.

26 There is as big a difference between beating and the occasional smack as there is between a drunken orgy and a small sherry.

There is no question that violence towards children is harmful. Research shows that children who are the victims of adult violence are more likely to bully, be violent towards other children, teachers and parents and grow up to be violent adults. They are also more likely to grow up to be adult victims, the wives of wife-beaters and the mothers of thugs. Children who witness violence between their parents and older siblings (and child-beating and partner-beating often go hand in hand) may also become violent themselves or become the victims of manipulative, violent and domineering children. Research suggests violence is especially harmful when it is gratuitous, when beatings have more to do with parental mood and whim than the child's behaviour.

The reasons are simple. Children copy what we do. The child's first port of call when faced with social relationships and social interactions is to play out the roles he sees his parents play. Because other children do not want to play with bullies,

60   The Golden Rules of Parenting

children who are the victims of violence tend to be thrown together into bands of tot thugs, junior thugs and, later, teenage and adult thugs and abusers.

However, this kind of violence is a far cry from a quick firm and single smack.

Using physical hurt as the first method of controlling other people's behaviour is not a good message to give a child. Nor does it work as a first-line method of control, as anyone who has witnessed over-zealous smackers can confirm. Smacking makes children resentful and angry, not cooperative and shamed. They feel self-righteous, defensive and vindictive, not sorry, ashamed or wanting to reaffirm a loving relationship.

But as a last resort many parents find a smack a useful way of telling the child 'Thus far and no further'.

When all else has broken down and there is nowhere else to go, it acts as a shock tactic and a demonstration that this time the child really has gone too far. The simple rule is that if a smack is not a shock and a surprise to the child, smacking is being used too frequently to be effective.

27 Think about why you are smacking. Is it to tell him he has completely overstepped the mark, or to pay back the hurt and disappointment his behaviour causes?

The first can work; the second just serves to make you feel better.

However smoothly families work, there are times when we are pushed to the edge by the defiant and unreasonable behaviour of children. We need to act swiftly to get things back in line. Some parents find it helpful to use smacks to indicate that the child has completely overstepped the mark. There is no evidence that occasionally smacking like this does any harm. A smack can stop the child in his tracks long enough to get things back into kilter. It's a first step. But while occasional smacks may have a role, frequent ones do not (by occasional here, we mean less than once a week). If you need to smack as a deterrent more often than this, smacking is clearly not giving results. Think carefully:

- Do you smack when you lose your temper or feel hurt?
- Is smacking as much about your emotions as his behaviour?

If the answer is yes, what you are teaching is that letting rip with your emotions is OK, which is often exactly what we are trying to stop.

If you are smacking too often, it is time to reconsider Rule 2: Children have a right to our love, to water, basic food and our protection, everything else must be earned. The rule means children do not get ice cream and Coke, TV, videos, trainers and fashionable clothes and birthday presents UNLESS something is received from them in return. That something is good behaviour, cooperation and adherence to family rules and values – or a step in that direction. Applying this rule is very tough on both child and parent, but it works.

- Being tough must be paired with love. Show it. Children get sympathy and empathy and understanding and all the love in the world. What is removed is indulgence.
- Their efforts must be appreciated and rewarded even when they do not succeed.
- They should be praised and rewarded for every tiny effort: *Jamie, it cannot have been easy to hold your temper with George, thank you. Let's get a takeaway, you choose.*

28 Ceremonial taps are a useful tool for the under-threes.

A toddler's attention is more easily gained by actions than words. So giving a little 'ceremonial tap' on the hand works well at this age. A ceremonial tap is a light smack to the hand that is not hard enough to hurt but firm enough to attract attention.

No! That's a naughty thing to do.
No, don't touch.
No, hot, that will hurt Sally.
No, dirty.
No, doggie will bite you.

Follow up the tap by getting down to the child's level, looking him in the eye and telling him what is wrong.

That's George's, not Sally's. George will be cross if you touch it. Shall we go and see what's in the toy cupboard for you?
Mummy would be sad if that broke. Let's put it in a safe place.

The younger the child, the more we need to attract his attention to get the message across – and the more often we need to repeat ourselves. Taps are not like smacks – a sign that discipline has broken down – but are a tool to help attract the child's attention. As such they can be used whenever you need to draw his attention to something important.

As the child grows up, and his language improves, he will be better able to understand and respond immediately to what we say. On occasions we still need to get down to his level and look him straight in the eye to make the point absolutely clear, but ceremonial taps probably become redundant by the time a child is about three and a half.

29 Everyone deserves to be first in line sometimes.

Everyone has the right to be first in the queue sometimes, and everyone has to accept a turn at the back. Sometimes the baby has to cry while you cuddle the toddler. Sometimes the toddler must wait while you finish dressing the baby. Sometimes both children have to wait while you give your partner a comforting hug and listen to the woes of the day.

Sometimes everyone has to hold back demands while the main caregiver takes care of herself.

If we leave all this to chance, it is inevitable that someone misses out, and the most likely person to miss out is the primary caregiver. Never having a turn causes stress and resentment and in time makes us feel we have lost ourselves in the mechanics of child-rearing and home-making.

Children thrive on structure. Make it clear that they each get their turn at being first, and they each have to wait.

Frankie, this is Freddie's time. He is first in line just now. It will be your time when the big hand points to the ceiling.

Sophie, let me just make this phone call and then I can read you that story.

Freddie, it is your turn to decide. Should we feed the ducks or go shopping first?

But remember that two minutes is an eternity for a toddler. Look up, give smiles, break off for a moment or two to give a word of encouragement.

30 Decide who owns the problem; if it only affects the child, it is his responsibility.

Seven is the age of reason – which means that this is the age when we should expect children to start to take responsibility for their actions. Why should a child remember his lunch box if he knows that someone else is prepared to run after him if he forgets?

He has better things to do with his time – and so do you.

So let go. This is his problem.

When the consequence of his actions affects no one but himself, the responsibility is the child's and his alone. So hand it over to him. Stand back, let him make mistakes and take the consequence. That is the only way he will learn. He will forget his lunch, his gym kit and where he put his library book unless he is forced to accept the consequences of his actions – only then will he take better note of where he leaves things. As long as you run after him, he will let you.

Problems that belong mainly to the child

- Getting to school on time.
- Doing his homework.
- Putting out his gym kit for washing.
- Putting his bike in the shed.
- Picking his CDs up off the floor.
- Remembering his lunch money and bus fare.
- Doing his music practice.

If he is sloppy he takes the consequences. School detentions, dirty gym kit and broken CDs.

It is hard on you as you watch your child skip into school without lunch, but if you find yourself reminding him everyday it is time to get tough. Usually one day without lunch is enough to ensure most children do the mental check that they have everything before they leave home.

Encourage him to do this by making your strategy transparent. Think aloud as you set off 'bag, keys, purse' as you get to the door each morning sets the pattern.

THE RULES OF LOVE

31 All children deserve their parents' love.

It is a child's right to be loved and it is our duty as parents to ensure that children are shown love. While they remain children, there are no exceptions to this rule. Children deserve hugs and kisses and words of love:

You are my little sunshine.
You are the very best Ruby in the whole world.
Oh Frankie, what a dreadful day I've had at work, I really need one of your special cuddles.

It is occasionally hard for a parent to love a particular child, and in times of stress and unhappiness it is hard for us to show love to anyone, including our children. Finding it hard to feel love does not negate our responsibilities to show love. If parents find this impossible in the short term, they should explain to the child:

Mummy is very sad today because Grandma is very ill.
Daddy has woken up very sad today, but even though I'm a
very sad Daddy, you are still my little darling.

If parents find it impossible in the long term, they should seek help.

We are often required in the course of our various duties to hide or even suppress our true feelings. If we can do it professionally, to please the customers, we can do it to protect the delicate unfolding of a small child's confidence and security. That is our responsibility. We are the grown-ups, and once we have children we have to behave as grown-ups. Of course it would be better for us to mean what we say when we say 'I love you', but children are hungry, and loving words (even if only half believed) mean a lot.

32 Let children know you love them and that you always will.

The smaller the child, the poorer the memory and the more likely he is to believe the surface message. If you show love, as far as he is concerned you mean love. If you are cross with him you have stopped loving him. If you have had reason to discipline a child, always let him know that you have forgiven and forgotten.

Don't just say 'I love you'; personalize the message:

Where is that little Jenny I love so much?
Who ever had a more special daughter?
You are the very best Freddie in the whole world.
What could be more beautiful than your smile?
Josie, that was great, come and give me a hug.

Inevitably, we sometimes do things that momentarily make our children feel less loved. The more love they have 'in the bank', however, the less these setbacks affect them. Bear in mind that if you had £5,000 in the bank, you would soon get over losing £1 of it, whereas if there was only £3 in the bank, you would probably brood about the loss of £1 all night.

33 Make the message 'I love you' clear to your children.

Ask almost any parent if they love their children and the answer is 'Yes.' Ask people if their own parents loved them, and it is not at all uncommon for people to feel that they did not. Clearly the message does not always get through.

Hugs and cuddles are the most obvious way of demonstrating love, but if you were raised to have a 'stiff upper lip', it will not come naturally. Being less demonstrative does not mean you love your child less, but it can sometimes feel that way. Preschoolers take things at face value, and the most obvious message wins.

Buying him the trainers he covets with the money that you had saved for your heart's desire is love, but it is not love that is necessarily recognized by a six-year-old. If after being angry with him you creep in to watch him sleep, that's love, but it's the anger, not love, that he will remember.

The Golden Rules of Parenting

If you find it hard to express physical affection, make sure you say 'I love you':

Jamie, I love you to bits.

Sarah, I hope you know I always love you.

You can also show love with a warm smile, obvious delight at seeing them, or just by letting them know they can come to you:

Oh, William, I'm so sorry, do you need a hug?

Always respect children's wishes. Don't just barge in:

I know it hurts, do you want to talk about it?

If you need a shoulder to cry on, I'm here.

But remember, hugs and kisses rarely go amiss.

34 Remember, love must grow and change with the child.

Love is shown to a child in many and subtle ways: in the provision of security, the 'buck stops here' sort of dependability; in the encouragement of independence; and ultimately in letting go. It is there in the bedtime story, the baking of his favourite cake, the smile across the room and the sympathy for his woes. Most of all it is there in our acceptance of him as a unique and lovable individual.

As we grow up it is these things, more than the words 'I love you', that convince us we are loved.

Preschoolers take love at face value. They only see one message. When you are happy together they feel love. When you are cross and they are angry they really do mean it when they say they hate you. It passes.

By the time they are six or seven, children are able to catch the subtle nuances of social interactions and see beyond the surface view. They begin to feel, as adults do, that love is a unique and special feeling 'from you to me and me to you', and that true love is unconditional and does not switch off. Being angry does not stop love.

As children grow towards puberty, they are also aware that love can smother, control and manipulate. That sometimes love is given in the best interests of the giver, rather than the receiver. Children now judge whether we love them, but also the quality of our love, and sometimes they find it wanting. They feel unloved, or that we only love them when they comply with the conditions they perceive we have placed on loving them.

Love is a way of life. Not just the words 'I love you'.

35 Don't smother their independence.

It is right and proper to cuddle a baby throughout the day, to tend to its every need and to watch its every move. Babies are helpless and dependent and need the constant care we give them, and it would be negligent for us to do otherwise.

They do not resent this love because they have no idea that our thoughts and feelings are entirely separate from theirs. All-embracing love cocoons them, makes them happy, and lets them grow.

But love that is appropriate at one time is not always appropriate at another. To carry on giving 'baby love' as children grow up stifles their development. Trees grow strong when they have their own sunshine. Children cannot develop in our shade. It is hard for a four-year-old who is still loved as if he was a baby to develop an emotional life that is separate from his parent, as every child must if he is to form good relationships outside the family.

The Golden Rules of Parenting

When love smothers emotional independence children find it hard to form mature relationships. If we refuse to change (by insisting on children being as dependent and unquestioning as small babies), they have two options:

- To accept the smothering and curtail independence, making it hard for them to form emotional relationships.
- To hide their emotional life and reject the smothering love and control.

Whatever the child does he loses; neither option is good. One curtails growth, and the other emotional independence. And growth and love are the lifeblood of childhood and life itself.

Gradually letting go of the 'baby' in your child is hard, but it is necessary if he is to reach emotional maturity. We have to allow children their independence and to stand back to love what they become.

36 You can also show love by letting go and allowing them to do things as they're ready.

Sometimes we need to stand back and ask ourselves what is best for the child, rather than what is easiest and best for us. It is not easy to let go, but it is always better to gradually relinquish control before children grab it from us. Which means that we must start letting them do things before it becomes obvious that they are ready.

Allowing independence is rather like making mayonnaise. At first we give responsibilities a drop at a time, making sure the child copes with each new freedom before the next arrives. After a while drops become steady drips, drips a steady stream.

It is much safer for the child to learn to cope with each new freedom before the next arrives. If independence is withheld until the child breaks through the dam (as he surely will), the flood of new freedoms will leave him vulnerable. He may not be able to cope, but will be reluctant to ask for help.

The Golden Rules of Parenting

You cannot keep a gate on the stairs for ever, hold his hand as he crosses the road at thirteen or remember his bus fare for him when he is at university. Love is allowing a child to gradually take over the responsibility for his own parenting bit by bit, step by step, until eventually he can manage perfectly well without you.

37 Love children for who they are, not what they do.

Small children take things at face value. If you say, 'Good boy, Tom' but never 'I love you, Tom', he may grow up believing he is only lovable if he is being good. Which is devastating when, inevitably, he falls from grace. The key here is to separate out that special Tom, who you love through thick and thin, from the things Tom does (which could be either good or bad).

The message comes in two parts. The first and most important is:

I love you because you are the most scrumptious, the most wonderful, the most lovable Tom anyone ever knew. What did I ever do to be such a lucky Mummy?

Which should not be confused with praising good behaviour:

Tom, I am very proud of how you behaved this afternoon. I know how hard it was for you to share your toys with Sophie. Frankie, I know you have tried your very best not to get cross with Tom today and I really appreciate that.

or criticizing bad behaviour:

Frankie, it upsets me to see you kicking Sophie. Kicking is not allowed. It is a very naughty way to behave.

38 Praise the behaviour AND love the child.

Good behaviour, even everyday good behaviour like being kind and helpful, deserves attention, appreciation and praise – and because praise rewards the child, giving praise and attention to good behaviours has the added advantage of making it more likely that the child will be good, kind and helpful again.

But be careful to balance praise with love. If you always praise her for being well behaved and never say, 'I love you', she may come to believe that she is only loved when she is good. Which would be sad.

As well as our praise of good behaviour, we should give smiles, kisses and hugs for nothing, for love, for free.

And so that there is never any confusion, always forgive and forget and make up after upsets. Let your child know that you never stop loving him, whatever he does.

Megan, I always love you, but I don't always love the things you do.

39 Children should know that they have our love by right; it will not be lost or gained because of what they do.

Parents know that however much their child hurts, upsets and disappoints them, they do not stop loving them. Parenthood puts love on a high wire without a safety net. At any moment it could come crashing down and our lives would never be the same again. That is the awesome thing about parenthood.

Deep down we always separate the emotion of love from the actions of our loved ones. We may hate what they do to us, but our heart tells us that whatever they do we cannot just switch off love.

It will always hurt as long as we still care.

It is not easy to get this message across to a child. To let him know that love prevails through all his naughtiness and all our exasperation, particularly if our fuse is short and our child wilful. The message 'I love you whatever you do' is particularly important for an insecure child, or one with a difficult temperament or behavioural problems. With such children we need to be especially careful how we express things.

The simple rule is that it must always be clear that we love the child, not the child's behaviour, and that we should criticize the child's behaviour, not the child.

Finally, always remember that there should be more 'My special Jamie' in any day's tally than 'that behaviour is unacceptable'.

40 Don't try to give equal love; love each child uniquely.

There is nothing finite about love. Every child brings his own suitcase of love into the world with him. We do not need to steal love from someone else in order to give it to this child, because the more we love, the more love we have to give.

Which is not always how we think or act. You wouldn't be the first parent to feel a twinge of jealousy when your child runs to the child minder and gives her a big sloppy kiss. Or the first parent to feel left out because their partner is besotted with the baby.

Is it any wonder that children are sometimes racked by jealousy and envy because they feel we love them less than we love their siblings? Every child watches for signs of favouritism, and inevitably they find them. By trying to be completely fair to each of our children, we simply draw attention to the inequalities.

Siblings know to the very last crumb which of them has the biggest slice of cake. If they measure fair shares of cake so accurately, what price the scales of love?

There is no point in saying 'I love you just as much' or 'I love you both the same', because as we all know, there really is a slice of cake that has that extra crumb. The more we try to deny this, the more we encourage children to check the deal they are getting.

Instead of striving to tell them your love for them is equal, strive to tell them that your love for each of them is unique. Don't say, 'Freddie, I love you just as much as I love Frankie.' Rather say, 'You are the very best Freddie in the whole wide world,' or 'You are my big boy with a freckly nose and I just love freckly noses to bits.'

41 Everyone is different. Give each child the type of love he needs.

Research suggests that something of what we are and what we need is there from the very start. Some children are born easy and sunny, others more difficult; some are shy, others more outgoing. Although there are fundamental rules about giving love to children, this does not mean there is a simple formula of how and how not to show it.

All parents need to find a way to express love that is true to themselves, and unique to each of their children. If she prefers a discussion on dinosaurs to cuddling up in front of the TV, this is what you should give her. If he needs a ten-minute cuddle and all she wants is a quick hug, so be it.

Everyone has his own style. Some of us are 'touchy-feely', others just smile from across the room. What you do with each child depends on the relationship between you. Be guided by his needs.

The only point to remember is that all children need love, and that very young children (and very upset children) understand direct demonstrations of love (such as cuddles and kisses) more easily than they understand words.

Patterns vary with need, and changes are often the first sign of problems. A demonstrative child who is suddenly withdrawn, or one who usually tolerates a quick hug who suddenly starts to cling is telling you something. Find out what.

THE NATURE OF CHILDREN

42 His expectation can be part of the problem – and most of the solution.

The smell of Christmas trees and tangerines, that first sight of the sea as you round that familiar bend. Such things have the power to elicit deep emotions. Sometimes without obvious reason you feel sad or afraid and most of the time you would be hard pressed to say exactly what had drawn up those old emotions – maybe it was the smell of paint or the shape of a tree. The only sure thing is that it is a blast from the past. It isn't just emotions that are elicited in this way. An aspirin cures your headache long before the chemicals have entered the blood stream. Mothers 'let down' milk minutes before the baby sucks the breast.

It's all in the power of anticipation, and it's a much more important control over behaviour than most of us imagine. Psychologists call it Pavlovian conditioning, after the man who first studied it. It is a basic form of learning that can occur with, or without, awareness. All that is needed is that one event consistently predicts what follows, like swallowing an aspirin predicts relief from the headache.

  The Golden Rules of Parenting

- If your child always sleeps in his cot (and never uses it for play) being put in his cot consistently and reliably precedes sleep. So being put into the cot makes him feel sleepy.
- If kissing his bumps better consistently and reliably precedes pain relief the kiss is the cure.
- If we always get angry with him at mealtimes, he is expecting that anger even before he sits down.

43 Get Pavlov on your side!

When food enters our mouth, we salivate. It is an automatic response that helps our digestive system work efficiently. Pavlov discovered that if a bell is rung just before food enters the mouth we salivate when we hear the bell. Similarly, we automatically close our eyelids when the wind blows into our eyes, and if we hear the rustle of trees before each puff of wind, we close our eyes as soon as we hear the sound.

It becomes completely automatic and most of the time we do not realize it is happening.

What this means is that if you consistently do certain things in the same way (such as having a regular routine for sleep), you can induce particular behaviours such as feeling sleepy 'to order'.

To get Pavlov on your side:

- Be selective. If your child NEVER uses his cot for daytime naps, he is more likely to sleep though the night when he goes to bed at night because the cot induces deep sleep rather than short naps.

- Be predictable. If you kiss him good night and walk away, he is more likely to associate your walking away with going to sleep. If you sing to him and stroke him, this is what he associates with dropping off to sleep, and he will want stroking at 3 a.m.

- Be consistent. Whatever you do, keep on doing it. It is the consistency and predictability with which A follows B that matters.

44 Routines help him to anticipate what follows.

A daily routine will help a child to anticipate what is about to happen – and that can, in turn, put him in the right frame of mind. (It's Pavlov again!)

- A certain routine before eating makes him feel hungry.
- A set routine leading up to bedtime makes him feel sleepy.
- A certain routine before settling down to a sustained activity puts him in a frame of mind that enhances concentration. So, for example, if you always do difficult things at a certain time, or in a certain place, he will be halfway there before he starts. The expectation hones him down to 'serious activity mode'. (This is why many people find it easier to concentrate when they are sitting at their desk.)

- Set a routine for comfort – a teddy to cuddle, a button sewn into his pocket so that he can touch it and think of you whenever he is worried, especially when you are not on hand.

Help set his biological clock

All animals have a biological clock, which makes them feel sleepier at certain times of day and more active at others. All humans sleep by night and are active by day. Within that daily pattern, most of us have an afternoon low. Babies need to set their clocks to ours. A regular routine (going to bed at a certain time, getting up at a certain time) helps them to do this, and to concentrate their main sleep into night-time.

Match activities to his clock

Most children find it easier to concentrate in the morning than in the late afternoon, and it is sensible to schedule more taxing activities into this slot. Mid afternoon is a time for relaxing activities, early evening a 'silly time' for boisterousness before calming down and going to sleep.

45 You can't expect him to structure his life unless you teach him how.

Even if we allowed them to, small children could not organize their own lives. They cannot put tasks in order, remember sequences, understand the flow of time, or plan more than one step ahead.

This does not mean they do not want order – everything we know about small children tells us that they are hungry for organization and predictability. If we gave most children a completely free choice, they would eat the same food and wear the same clothes every day. They like to drink from 'their cup', sit in 'their place', watch the same video and get us to read the same story over and over again.

Why? Because it is the constant elements of a child's life that help him to remember what has gone before, how to do something, and what to expect. It is this that makes him feel secure.

- Regularity sets up expectations and helps rid him of distractions.
- It sets a pattern for his early years that can be carried forward.
- Because structure makes children feel secure, those with well-structured lives are less likely to cling to us in order to feel safe. Which allows us a little time for ourselves.
- Although we should impose structure on small children, we need gradually to hand over the responsibility for structuring their lives to the children themselves as they grow up.

46 Don't let Pavlov work against you!

You can get Pavlov to work for you – or you can get him to work against you. The conditioning process is usually unconscious and often unintended which all too often means that we unwittingly let it work against us.

Letting Pavlov work against us at mealtimes

If mealtimes are a constant battleground, the child feels stressed even before the food is in front of him. For some, stress causes a craving for sweet foods. For others, it turns off hunger. In all cases stress makes the child angry and upset and disrupts eating and digestive processes. Some children respond by just eating pudding. Some eat almost nothing while they are at the table (and under stress), but feel hungry as soon as they get down from the table and the stress has been removed. Which can be infuriating to parents. It may seem as if they are deliberately provoking us; but they are not.

The ritual of worry on your part and stress on theirs is going nowhere. You are the only one who can initiate change. So change. Stop worrying and just let him eat what he wants for a month or two. He can get all his goodness from milk (flavoured if necessary), but add a vitamin supplement if it makes you feel better. Change the cues that turn on stress. Have meals in the garden, or picnics at a small table in the lounge; get a tablecloth and a special plate. Now start again, and very gradually introduce a more balanced diet. (See Rule 95.)

Letting Pavlov work against behavioural change
If people expect a child to cry or lose his temper and tiptoe around his emotional volatility he will feel a surge of emotion as soon as there is any sign that we expect him to lose control. In the same way that if we expect failure we make it more likely, if we expect success we help him succeed. If we are afraid of heights, spiders or mice, he can catch that fear because of the uneasiness he feels when we are uneasy. If people expect him to be naughty, disruptive and aggressive, he can catch that feeling too.

Good or bad conditioning can make our expectations come true.

47 Never underestimate how much stress can affect our behaviour – and theirs.

Stress has widespread effects on people's health and happiness. When stressed, we are more likely to have accidents, and because immunity is low we are more susceptible to illnesses like colds and flu. Stress makes us prone to anger, anxiety and depression, we forget things, and we find it harder to concentrate or get organized. Stress upsets children in similar ways, and because, compared to adults, they are less able to control emotions, concentrate, or sustain attention, stress can produce quite serious behavioural problems.

Most small children experience many major changes in their short lives: a new baby, an older sibling starting school, parents returning to work. But stress is not just caused by such major traumas; the cumulative effects of daily hassles also cause it. Small children are very dependent on familiar physical and social environments to feel secure, and any changes in these, or their daily routines, are stressful. High days and holidays are potentially problematic.

Is it any wonder that they are sometimes unhappy, angry and badly behaved, and there are days when they do not concentrate, or organize their thoughts and feelings? If this frustrates us, and that frustration shows, we make things worse. It is very easy for us both to enter a downward spiral where we increase each other's stress levels. Children cannot see their own way out of this, which means that we have to do it for them, however difficult that is.

48 Recognize that your child will not always tell you what is wrong.

Well, did you always tell your own parents? As we grow up, most of us don't – even when there are quite serious things to tell. Parents know what happens to small children because they constantly watch them. If we didn't see what happened someone else did. Once children start school, they are out of our sight and control. We can't initiate conversations about school because we do not know where to start.

Causes of stress in the early school years

- Problems with school work. Studies suggest that behavioural problems, such as school disruption, hyperactivity and aggression, often begin after children start to fail; that is, the child is having difficulty learning to read, playing sports or coping with simple activities such as dressing, or controlling a pen. Children with dyslexia and apraxia (clumsy child syndrome) are more likely to be disruptive and unhappy at school.

- Problems with peers. As many as one child in four does not have a close friend at school. It's a long day to be alone.

- Problems with teasing. Children can be, and are, very cruel to each other. When a child does not know how to cope, and especially when he has no friends to support him, teasing can get completely out of hand.

- Problems with bullying. Schools should have policies on bullying, and most do. But that does not mean that they always stop it, ensure it does not happen, or deal with it when it does.

- Problems at home. You may think that you are hiding it from him, but it is unlikely that you are. The older the child the more serious is the upset when parents split up, or when they quarrel. Do not underestimate the stress on him, or how long it will last.

49 Deal with stress and the consequences of stress.

- Try to remove the cause of stress; if this is impossible, be forgiving. Ignore what can be ignored.
- Set and keep limits. It will not help the child if you allow or encourage bad behaviour. Remember you also show care by caring what he does.
- Keep to a routine, stay calm and reduce the level of stimulation by turning down any excess noise.
- Help him relax; massage, cuddles, a comforter, a hot bath, soft lighting and gentle music all help.
- Show children how to vent anger by kicking cushions, and how to lift their spirits by saying 'Cheese, cheese and more cheese, please' (putting the facial muscles into a smile really does help).
- If he is restless, encourage him to do something physical – letting off steam helps him calm down.

- Stress makes it difficult to concentrate or pay attention and this is likely to make him disruptive. If he needs to concentrate, remove any distractions. Put away toys, turn off the TV and radio. Removing distractions helps older children organize their thoughts and feelings.

Try to understand and help them express their feelings:
  I know you sometimes wish we didn't have a baby.

Let children know it is OK to feel angry:
  It is all right to feel fed up with William.
  It's OK to be angry that your dad and I are quarrelling.
  It's OK to worry about it; I'm worried too.

Explain why it is not possible to change things:
  But Dad and I just can't find a way of being together.

And find a solution for the moment:
  I suggest that you call the red cushion 'Mum' and the blue one 'Dad' and give us both a good kick.

50 Children have to let off steam. Help them to do it as happily and constructively as possible.

The car stops and out they hop, jumping, pushing, being silly. It's sometimes called the popcorn effect, after the way popcorn bursts when you heat it in a pan. This sudden bursting into action is something all small animals do.

Why?

Well one suggestion is that it is necessary for the normal development of muscles and bones. Scientists who have examined how animals move in these ways say that the pattern of activity is remarkably like the optimal training patterns athletes use.

The main thing to remember is that letting off steam cannot be avoided – and if you try to constrain children, they become restless, and stop paying attention. If this sort of activity is suppressed in animals, they become permanently hyperactive and find it difficult to attend or do things systematically.

So allow children time to let off steam every few hours. Chase them around the sofa, get out the trampoline (or jump off the steps), go and stamp in puddles, chase falling leaves, run around the block – but do it.

51 Sometimes he will need to vent his excitement before you can calm him down.

Wind him up . . .

- Put on a certain piece of music and chase him around the room.
- Dance together; shout out loud or jump up and down on the spot. If you do this often enough (and especially if the music is special), you will find that he starts to run around as soon as he hears the opening bars of his 'wild music'.
- Children fidget if they have to sit still for long. If he is getting restless put on the music and join him (wild behaviour needs company).
- Children get restless when out shopping or in waiting rooms and other places where 'wild' behaviour is not possible. A good boost of activity before you get into the shops will help. Try shouting under bridges, running around the park.

The Golden Rules of Parenting

- If children get too restless, they cannot concentrate. Always precede a sustained activity with a period of 'wild' activity, even if they are not yet fidgeting.

. . . in order to calm him down.
- Turn off the music, TV and any extraneous noise.
- Talk face to face, getting down to his level if necessary.
- Children find it easier to concentrate on the task in hand if there is no competition. When he looks up, he should not see lots of other things he could do.

Find things to do when there is nothing for him to do: take a story tape and earphones to the waiting room; play 'I Spy' when you are in the supermarket; think of the silliest hats you could wear.

52 A young child's attention is easily captured.

For preschool children, vision usually wins out. What he is looking at tends to dictate what he thinks and what he does. If a child looks up from what he is doing and sees something new (or different), he can easily be distracted from one activity into a whole new train of thought.

If the floor is scattered with toys, he will find it hard to concentrate on any one of them. This is because every time he looks up from his game, there is a danger he will see (and think about) something else he could do. Whenever there are distractions, there is a danger that his attention will be captured. Remember, he can only think about one thing at a time.

The simple lesson here is that if you want a child to concentrate, put away the distractions.

- Don't leave toys scattered about when he needs to concentrate.
- Use a cupboard rather than shelves to store toys, so that he is less easily distracted by other things he might do.
- Let him sit so he has his back to the room, use local rather than room lighting.

Noise can also distract, because his eyes will be drawn towards the source of any sound.

- Turn off the radio and TV.
- If you need to talk to him, disrupting his concentration, redirect him to the activity by looking at it and commenting on it.

53 Small children find it harder to stop what they are already doing than to keep going.

And the more they are aroused, the harder they find it to stop.

When a baby is born, his brain is not yet fully developed. What is present is specialized to control his current needs – to do things like breathing or urinating rather than to modify how or when he does such things.

At first it is as if he only has the 'on' switch. He stops feeding because he falls asleep, he stops crying because he is picked up, and he stops smiling because he no longer hears your voice or sees your face.

As his brain develops (it more than doubles in size) he begins to learn how to stop or modify these 'go' responses. He learns to hold his breath, and match his breathing to his actions, to whimper or cry vigorously, to refuse to eat whether hungry or full, and to urinate when he gets to the toilet.

That pattern of 'go ' before 'stop' persists. Children learn to walk before they learn how to stop, to run in a straight line before they can turn corners. One of the consequences of this is that it is much easier for a child to 'go' than to 'stop' – the more aroused and excited he is, the more likely he is to switch over to all systems go.

Which is one reason why he loses control.

STAYING IN CONTROL

54 Accept the child you have; don't keep wishing he were someone else.

There is nothing more conducive to feeling unloved than growing up knowing you are not the child your parents wanted. Not pretty or clever or sporty – in their eyes simply not up to scratch. It can be equally hard to be their perfect girl with the golden curls who grew up to be their very special princess – but who also feels her life has been sacrificed to her parents' blind ambition.

It is natural and proper to be ambitious for our children, to guide them along the right paths, to make opportunities for them when we can, and to help them make the most of those opportunities. But there is a fine line between opening up the possibilities and shoe-horning children down predetermined routes. Children should not have to be special to be special to us. To the outside world a child can be mediocre in every respect, but if he can draw love from the people who matter most to him, he is a success. A child can be special in every respect, but if he fails to draw love from the people who matter, he may feel a total failure.

The Golden Rules of Parenting

Always let a child know he is special because of who, not what, he is.

Tom, you are such a special boy to me.

And that you are proud of his efforts:

Tom, I am proud of how hard you have worked at this.

And his achievements, whether great:

I was so excited to see you racing towards the line.

or small:

We must ring Grandma Robinson and tell her you came second in the sack race.

55 Don't turn acceptance into indulgence.

Lucy has a bad temper. And everyone knows that Lucy's temper can spoil the day. Push her the wrong way and she can sulk for England. When Lucy is in a mood, everyone tiptoes around her. So is it any surprise she often sulks and gets her way? There is no suggestion here that Lucy is deliberately manipulative. She is simply doing what her family has taught her to do.

Lucy genuinely finds it hard to keep her emotions under control. Her moodiness lasts longer these days, because when she has felt sad and unhappy in the past (as she does when she loses her temper) people have made her feel better by paying attention to her moodiness. It's a simple learning process.

It is very easy to train a child to be a prima donna without being aware that we are doing so. Just as it is easy for a child to learn how to be a prima donna without understanding what it is he has learned. He acts without any deliberate intention of manipulating; we reward him without any intention of encouraging him.

If we excuse bad behaviour because a child is 'gifted', 'easily upset', 'difficult', 'emotional', 'on a short fuse', 'artistic', 'special' or 'temperamental', we simply prolong his problems.

56 Avoid labelling your child.

If George kicks the door as he goes into the room, it is easy to jump to the conclusion that the fight with his brother that breaks out shortly afterwards is his doing. That when his little brother cries it is because George gave him an entirely unprovoked punch. We hate to admit it, but it is this sort of behaviour that makes us think he is a bully.

The label means that no one stands back and asks what really happened. Maybe this time George was entirely innocent. He just came in to watch TV and innocent put-upon James seized the opportunity to get in a good kick and then yelled for all he was worth before George could hit back. James wins because our labels (George bully, James victim) stop us from asking questions.

It is easy to find labels for our children. Whether it's the shy one, the clever one, the sporty one, the difficult one, the labels colour our perceptions. More alarmingly, they colour children's perceptions of themselves. In time children grow into their labels – as the following famous experiment shows.

Teachers in the USA were told that one group of students were clever and another group rather dim (although there were in fact no differences between the two groups). By the end of the school year, both groups of children were living up (or down) to their labels. The 'clever' children had achieved more academic success than the 'dim' ones.

- Instead of saying 'You are a bully', say 'Hitting your brother is unacceptable'.
- Instead of saying 'You won't be able to do that', say 'It's hard and I am proud of you for trying'.
- Instead of saying 'James is the clever one', say 'James does very well at school'.

It is always the behaviour that should be labelled, not the child.

57 Enable your child.

A label says the way it is and tells the child there is no point in trying.

Remember she's handicapped.
Don't upset Charles, I need some calm.
He's very sweet, but not very bright.
She's too fat.
Why are you always so naughty?
Why can't you just try once in a while?

There are lots of ways of labelling a child and running him down to himself and to others. Sometimes we do it without ever realizing. But that does not mean that the child misses the message. We do not have to call him stupid for him to feel stupid.

I'll do that for you, you'll never manage.
You know you can't do that, look at the mess you have made.

He's much smaller than you, make allowances.
She's pretty and that's what matters most for a girl.

But by the same token we do not have to call him capable to make him feel enabled.

You did your best, and I'm proud of you.
Hey, that's difficult and you are doing so well.
It is very hard, even big boys find it difficult.

It is amazing what we can do if we believe it is possible. When girls felt they were not as bright as boys were, they were rarely top of the class. Now they have been told differently, they outstrip boys in all public exams. A generation ago, no one would have believed that anyone in a wheelchair could become an athlete.

How wrong they were.

58 Forgive and forget.

Toddlers soon forget. They can fall on the floor in an uncontrollable rage, and yet be up and smiling five minutes later. When it is over it's over, and there is no guilt and rarely any grudges. Forgiving and forgetting are not particularly important at this age because unless we tell them otherwise toddlers act as if we have forgiven them anyway.

By three, children are beginning to feel sad and sorry for themselves after they have behaved badly. Anger and upset is followed by a period when the child feels bad. He needs our forgiveness to find closure. By five, children can be moody and difficult without any obvious reason, and sometimes seem as if they are courting upset. They can feel guilt and seek revenge.

Without forgiveness negative moods like this often persist with all the negative effects that has on their subsequent behaviour, and their ability to keep their emotions in check. Research suggests that if children are not forgiven when they behave badly or lose control, they are more likely to misbehave again.

If your child behaves badly, describe what happened:

> *I see one very angry boy who threw his toys all over the room.*

Accept what happened without condoning it:

> *I know it is difficult not to lose your temper; building is difficult. But throwing toys is dangerous and it is not allowed.*

Help him to solve the problem:

> *Now let's pick up the bricks and put them away.*

Forgive and forget:

> *Let's try and forget all those angry feelings. I'll make us a drink and then we can cuddle and make up.*

59 Find something good to say about what they do.

Everyone is sometimes critical, but for some, constant criticism is a way of life. Over the years the nearest and dearest of such carpers probably learn that this is their way of caring, but not everyone understands this and it is not an easy message for small children to decipher.

'Nothing was ever good enough for my parents' is a common accusation of grown-up children. Few of us are immune. Ask anyone to make a list of their good points, and the list is almost always short, while a list of their bad points is usually much longer. Does this self-criticism get us anywhere? Make us happy? Reduce stress or help us lead a good and productive life?

Of course not.

So why project self-criticism on to children as if it were a virtue? When society was structured so most of us deferred to our 'betters', deep-seated humility was a necessary tool for keeping the unwashed hordes in line. It is no longer like that – or shouldn't be. Self-confidence and self-worth are not recipes for bragging or arrogance; we only need to brag if we feel deeply uncertain of our worth.

Find something positive to say. It does a child no harm to know that whatever strangers think about him, his family believes he is very, very special indeed. That whatever he achieves or fails to achieve his nearest and dearest know his true worth.

If it's good, say so:

That's great, Jamie.

and if it isn't so great (and he knows), find something good to say:

Well, it's not quite up to your usual standard, but that's a really pretty flower you drew in that corner.

rather than saying:

That's just a sloppy effort, you are capable of doing a lot better.

Carrots work better than sticks, and the best carrots are those he provides for himself.

60 Keep a tally of praise and criticism – and always let praise win.

No one comes into the world knowing right from wrong. Children are taught what is good and what is bad behaviour. Like everything else a small child learns, it needs practice. Which is fine when he is working out how to be good, but a pain when he is working out what is naughty. Because bad behaviour is hard to ignore, we tend to give it more attention. It's easy to criticize more than we praise.

Can't you two go for ten minutes without quarrelling?
Do you have to make so much mess?
Stop making that stupid noise.
Get your coat on NOW before I lose my temper.

And what is there to praise? They got dressed – or nearly dressed. They ate their breakfast – or most of it. They could have got all the toys out but confined themselves to a single drawerful. Even when they are exceptionally good, their behaviour does not grab us in quite the same way. Indeed, we often ignore children while they are good, because such times

  The Golden Rules of Parenting

offer a period of calm to get on with our own needs. Especially if we have a difficult or badly behaved child.

Unless we make a concerted effort our criticism of the child's behaviour invariably outweighs the praise. A negative state of affairs that can leave the child feeling he cannot get anything right.

And if he can't get anything right, why should he try?

Aim at least to balance the scales of criticism and praise – better still, set aside a few days when you ensure that you always keep the tally of praise higher than the tally of criticism. You'll be surprised at how well this works.

61 Sometimes they have to wait while you do what's important to you.

Sometimes everyone has a right to be at the front of the queue. And that includes parents. It does a child no favours to allow him to grow up thinking the world stops every time he says 'I want'. Success today is more and more dependent on networking and social skills, and that means everyone should know when to push themselves forward and when to stand back. It does children no harm to imbibe this with their mother's milk.

Which is one very good reason why you must sometimes say 'It's my turn, my time, and you will just have to wait.' A far more important reason is that parents have rights. The days when mothers were supposed to be selfless are, thankfully, over. There is no need for you to feel guilty about sometimes asking the children to wait while you do something for yourself. Even if that something is quite unnecessary and indulgent.

In your time it is your choice.

The Golden Rules of Parenting

If you want your children to treat you with respect you have to demand that respect. Indulging children is not the way to do it. Respect comes from self-esteem, and it's hard to hang on to self-esteem when you are always the doormat to your family. It would be wrong and selfish to always put yourself first. Like all things, there is a balance.

HOW TO TREAT
CHILDREN

62 Criticize the behaviour, not the child.

When a child behaves badly, the most natural response is to call him names.

You bad boy!

You wicked child!

You little horror, you devil, you silly fool, I can't believe you could be so stupid.

What we really mean is that his naughty, dangerous or wilful behaviour makes us angry and upset, and that this behaviour is totally unacceptable to us. So why not tell the truth and say how you feel?

When you talk to me like that it makes me very angry.

I am sad that you chose to lie to me.

Say that the behaviour is unacceptable:

In this house we do not speak to each other in that rude, disrespectful way.

I will not tolerate stealing.

Pass judgement on the behaviour by all means, and punish it if you feel it is appropriate to do so, but do not say and do not imply that a child is wicked, bad or unlovable or that you have stopped loving him because of what he has done. Describe feelings, criticize and punish bad behaviour but never suggest that your love is contingent on his good behaviour, or that because he behaves badly he has become a bad person.

63 Don't try to treat them equally; treat each child uniquely.

In a perfect world everyone would be equal, and one advantage would be neatly balanced against some disadvantage. But that is not how it is. As we know only too well, some people have more than their fair share of brains, beauty, wealth, health and happiness – and they get all the perks that are going too. It could certainly be fairer but it can never be equal.

Even within the family, equality for all is an unworkable ideal. By striving to treat children equally we simply draw attention to the fact that we have failed to deliver. There is no way a cake can be cut into two exactly equal portions (even if we counted all the crumbs, the children would say that some crumbs were worth more than others).

- You cannot buy gifts that have exactly the same value to each child. Buy according to need, or because you see something that is exactly right for one child. Do not feel that you need to give to each child every time.

  The Golden Rules of Parenting

- Next time you feel like giving a present, buy for one of the other children. Over time you should strive to be fair.
- Treat children uniquely – if one child needs more attention this week, give it, but be ready to give to the other children in their hour of need. You cannot give exactly the same amount of attention, but you can try to give what each child needs.
- In the real world everyone has to learn how to deal with being at the back of the queue. It needs practice.
- Even those children who need lots of help gain by becoming more independent. Allow them to.
- Love uniquely. Love each child for who they are – and show that love in the way each child needs you to show it.

64 Jealousy is perfectly normal.

We can help what we do but we cannot help what we feel. It is normal and natural for small children to sometimes feel jealous of each other.

Let children know that it is all right to feel jealous:

That must be upsetting.

I expect you feel cross about that.

Gemma, I know Mummy is often very busy with William, and that you sometimes feel left out. I'd be upset if you were sometimes too busy for me.

Describe the situation:

It's a difficult problem. William has a dirty nappy and you need me to finish the story.

It's hard not to be upset when Grace spends so much time with Olivia.

The Golden Rules of Parenting

Find a way of expressing the emotion:

Do you want to draw me a picture of how you feel?

Do you want to talk about it?

Stamp to show me how cross you feel about this . . . That much? That's very cross.

Help him to find a solution:

What do you think should be done?

Should I make William wait or should we settle him first so we get more time to ourselves?

Perhaps Jamie will let you borrow the pens if you let him use your remote-control car. Why not ask him?

Comfort him with a cuddle, but do not reward or excuse bad behaviour.

I know you are upset, but that is no excuse for hitting your sister. Go to your room and when you feel sorry for what you have done, come down and we will talk about it together.

65 Children always squabble. You can't avoid fights, but you can reduce them.

Children are born with a single-track mind. They want it and they want it now – and it does not matter one iota what the rest of us want.

They have to learn the rules of communal living: about ownership, rights and mutual respect. They have to be shown how to be considerate, to negotiate rather than grab, and that we approve when they are helpful and kind.

They also have to learn how to cope with competition. In real life, competitors do not always play fair. To get what he wants a child may have to be pushy, deceitful, overpowering, manipulative, aggressive and ready to take advantage at every opportunity. That is what real competition is about.

Children need to know when cooperative tactics work best, and when competitive tactics would be a better option, when it is safe to compete and when it is best to stand back and let others get on with it. Such things are best learned in the safety of the family, in games and sibling rivalries, in play fights, competitions for attention, and real arguments and fights. Which is why siblings quarrel and fight.

Fighting cannot be avoided. However, it can be reduced.

- Treat each child uniquely; stop trying to treat them equally.
- Do not give in to manipulation or bad behaviour.
- Do not reward squabbles by giving them attention or by getting drawn into arguments or fights.
- Have simple house rules about property ownership and the rights children have over their rooms and beds. If it's her bed, she can say who can sit on it.
- Expect children to sort things out – after all, this is what they are trying to learn when they fight.
- Look for the flash points and try to steer clear of them.

66 Don't get drawn into their fights.

All children fight. They fight about important things, they fight about silly things, and sometimes they just fight for no obvious reason. Research suggests that those things that cause children the most upset will, a few years hence, be the very things that they are most grown-up about.

On average, children of the same gender fight more often than those of different genders, and boys fight more than girls do. But individual personalities also play a role. Some children fight more than others do. Others are angels at home and horrors at nursery and school – and vice versa. If parents are argumentative, children tend to copy.

Don't get drawn in. If they are winding each other up, put on a poker face and walk away. If you join in, it will escalate. If they try to draw you in, say, 'I have confidence you can sort this one out without me.' If they try to involve you again, just leave the room.

If things are getting out of hand, describe what you see:

Have I got this right? Frankie, you want to play with George's car, but George, this is your car and you do not want Frankie to use it.

Help them find the solution:

Frankie, George can say who plays with his toys. That is the rule. But if George isn't using the car, he might let you borrow it. Perhaps you could lend him something of yours. I have confidence that you can sort this out.

If the temperature is rising fast, separate the children and impose conditions for returning:

You can come back when you have cooled down.

If they come to blows:

No hitting, that's the rule. Both go to your rooms at once.

67 Never accept violence.

No one can help how they feel – but they can help how they act.
If your child is angry, describe what you see:

I know that you wanted to go to the cinema tonight, and that
you are angry that we cannot go.

Accept anger, and allow it to be expressed.

It is all right to feel angry.
It is all right to tell people you are angry with them.
If you are angry, you can say a rude word.

But do not allow aggression to be directed at other people.

You can shout out loud but not at other people.
You can say a rude word but you cannot call someone a rude
name.
You can kick the cushion, but not your sister.

Let them take responsibility for their actions:

Jamie, in this house we say that whoever hits or kicks is in the wrong. You know the rules.

It does not matter what Frankie did; there is never any excuse for hitting. Go to your room until you have calmed down and then I expect you to apologize.

Frankie, take off Jamie's T-shirt at once, then go and wash it. You will find the soap powder under the sink. You should not take Jamie's things without his permission.

If they do as they are told:

Thank you for that.

It is hard to do the right thing and I am proud that you did.

And if they do not:

I will not ask you again, Jamie. I am going to count to three. If you have not done as I asked by the time I finish, your computer must be turned off for twelve hours. One, two, three . . .

If you threaten you must carry it through – so be careful what you say.

68 Never threaten what you will not or cannot carry through.

Sometimes we make threats that we cannot possibly carry out.

Josh, if you do not shut up I'll put you out of the car at the next bus stop.

If I hear one more cross word from you two, Christmas is cancelled.

If you don't bring me your clothes to pack, you will not come on holiday.

Sometimes we threaten sanctions that are too stiff to carry through.

You will get no pocket money for the rest of the year.

I'm going to take that computer back to the shop.

We'll have to sell your bike to pay for it.

  The Golden Rules of Parenting

After the first few times (when he might have thought you meant it), he will just shrug his shoulders and think 'There she goes, overreacting again.' Because you threaten too much, you cannot carry the punishment through, and no one takes any notice.

Never threaten if you do not intend to carry it through. Empty threats just undermine your authority.

69 Don't keep making threats: act.

If you always threaten a child five times before you act, there is no point in him responding until the fifth time. All such threats do is undermine your authority by encouraging him to carry on doing what he wants to do for a few more minutes.

Instead of threatening, warn:

Sally, I am going to need the table in ten minutes, so you should think about finishing that picture or putting it somewhere safe until later.

Just finish up now because it's almost bedtime.

Count down:

When the big hand's on the five, you should start clearing up.

Are you watching that clock?

Time now. I'm just going to put the pasta on, so we need the table clear. Could you do it now, please?

Don't accept prevarication. Act.

Sally, I cook your supper and I expect you to be helpful in return. Now clear that away at once.

No arguments, do it now.

You are not allowing the dinner on to the table. If we cannot use the table, you will have to go to bed without supper. It's your choice.

Follow through:

Thank you for your cooperation.

I see you have chosen to go to bed without supper.

70 It's not deliberate; in the face of temptation, small children often forget the rules. They can often get carried away through over-excitement.

What they see and hear dominates small children. What they know comes a poor second. Whatever the rules, and however well he knows them, a child can be completely stolen away by temptation.

However many times you tell him not to run into the road, he will chase the ball because just at this moment he has a one-track mind. He knows he should not poke his baby sister with his toy sword, but when he feels cross and jealous he is blind to what is right and wrong in the situation.

Often such things have only a passing importance, but sometimes 'leaping before they look' can have tragic consequences.

Small children need our eyes and ears to protect them, because they really cannot do it themselves.

We have to think ahead for them, because they are often incapable of seeing where their actions will lead them.

71 Always distinguish communal property from personal property. And remember that it's not communal while someone is using it.

They can all share the play dough because you made it for them all to use, and the felt tips because you bought the new pack for them all to share. But the bike is Georgie's bike, and that means she can say who is allowed to use it.

The following simple property rules save arguments.

- If you do not own it, you must ask before using it.
- If you don't want people to use your things, you can say so.
- If you are not using it, or lending it out to someone else, you must put it away. Flaunting is not allowed.
- If you give toys away, or put them into the communal pile, you cannot just grab them back when you want to; a change of ownership gives away property rights.

- To avoid arguments about any change of ownership, write down all changes and get both children to sign (a thumbprint will do).

- Because something is communal property does not mean you can grab it whenever you want. While Sarah is using the red pen, it becomes hers. After she finishes using it, it goes back into communal ownership. If Sophie then takes it, it is hers while it remains in use.

- It helps if you put a limit on how many pens (Lego pieces, balls of play-dough) a child can be said to be using at any one time.

Remember, young children define themselves by what they can do and what they own. At three she is 'the little girl with the red coat and the blue bike'. When someone takes her bike, they take a little bit of her.

72 Don't jump to conclusions. They may not be as guilty (or as innocent) as you think.

We see what we see – and sometimes all we see is what children want us to see. As we understand it, the elder one hit the younger. We didn't see – but we know he often hits out in that mood. So comfort the little one and send the older one to his room.

But is that all it was?

Could it be that the little one deliberately engineered that thump by poking out his tongue and kicking his brother's car across the room? With his brother in disgrace he gets your undivided attention. It may not be like this every time (or this time), but your youngest would be a very unusual child if he did not sometimes take advantage. Children learn to repeat actions that are rewarded, whether or not they are aware of the contingencies.

The lesson is:

- ● Keep an open mind.
- ● Try and avoid taking sides.
- ● Keep a good look-out for crocodile tears.
- ● Watch children when they do not think you can see them.
- ● Don't rush in too quickly to protect the younger child; tell them you expect them to sort out problems for themselves.
- ● Make it clear to the older child that there is never any excuse for hitting.
- ● Praise the older child whenever he keeps his temper in the face of provocation – and whenever he manages to get through the hour, morning or day without upset. If it's a problem, try using a star chart to reward BOTH children if they do not fight.

73 Encourage children to stick up for themselves.

All parents worry about bullying – and so they should. Victims of bullying can be thrown into such despair that they attempt to kill themselves – and sometimes succeed. While it is never the victim's fault, some children are more likely to be victimized.

- Never encourage a child to play the victim. Patterns of behaviour that are safe (and give advantage) within the family can lead to disaster when played out outside.
- Don't jump to conclusions. When dealing with your children, never assume that one of them is innocent and the other guilty. It is rarely this clear-cut.
- Expect children to sort out disagreements themselves. If you always jump in to sort out the youngest one's problems, you encourage him to play the victim.

Teach strategies

When children quarrel, describe what is wrong, accept anger and tell them you expect them to sort out the problem. If the younger one is being bullied, teach him to repeat what is being said:

> *Fish face!*   *YOU say I'm a fish face.*
> *You wet your pants!*   *YOU say that I wet my pants.*

This avoids confrontation but is suitably irritating without accepting what is being said.

An older (and bolder) child might say:

> *You believe I'm a fish face, and that's fine by me, you're free*
> *to think what you like. I don't believe I'm a fish face and that*
> *is all that matters.*

A more timid or younger child might just look as unconcerned as they can and say 'oh yes!' regardless of what is being said. Show children how to put on an expressionless face; bullying is not much fun if the victim does not react. Make a game of it. Teach him to look into the middle distance, take a deep breath, hold his head up, open his eyes wide and say 'Oh' (it gets the face into a fairly neutral pose).

74 Never make comparisons between children: compare his behaviour (or achievement) with something he has done on a separate occasion.

Why would any child want to enter into a competition he could not win if his efforts were always compared unfavourably with someone else's?

Always treat each child as a unique individual who is trying his best. If you do, they are more likely to try to live up to your expectations.

Sally, I know you did your best, and I am proud of you.

You worked so hard and you did your best and that is what matters most.

The way to expect improvement is to make comparisons with the child's own performance, not with the behaviour of another child.

> Sam, that is OK, but it is not your best effort. I expect you to try a bit harder next time.
>
> Susie, this is not nearly as good as last time. What happened?
>
> Sally, you were nearly there. If you practise I know you will be able to do it.
>
> Steve, you are so close, perhaps by next week you will be able to manage it!

Never, never:

> Jenny is so much better than you are at this.
>
> Tim can do it, I don't see why you can't make a bit more effort.
>
> We are going to keep on doing this until you can do it as well as Jodie.

Appreciate effort, rather than success.

> I really appreciate how hard you have tried today.
>
> I am proud of the effort that you have put into that.
>
> Nearly there, I am confident you will make it.
>
> You are doing so well.

75 Don't bad-mouth.

It is between the two of you and it is not anyone else's business. So if your child has behaved badly, tell him so. If you are disappointed, let him know. But do not go bad-mouthing him to anyone prepared to listen, nor allow others to join in the chorus when you discuss his behaviour with him. It is nothing to do with them.

Of course you sometimes need to ask advice, or tell your partner or friends there are problems. But it is possible to do this when the child and your other children cannot overhear you and without running the child down.

Children imitate us; they say what we say and do what we do. If there is open season on criticizing one child, you can be certain the others will join in.

A few simple rules help here.

- Never bad-mouth – whatever he has done, the rule is that you describe and criticize behaviour, not individuals.
- Never impute motivation. You do not know, nor do they.
- Never join in or allow others to join in. Put a child on the defensive and he becomes self-righteous. He no longer feels in the wrong – he feels wronged (and to some extent he is right).
- Don't moan about one child to another.
- Don't let a child hear you moaning about him to someone else.
- Never call him names.
- Never let others call him names.
- If you want to tell him, do so to his face.

How to Treat Children **167**

76 It's much safer to allow independence to develop gradually.

When we let go (which we must do sooner or later), our children will go through a vulnerable patch until taking responsibility for their own safety and self-preservation has become second nature. Until being careful has slipped from conscious awareness (where it is exposed to distraction) into the preconscious automatic mode (where distraction is much less likely), children are in danger.

When we first learn to drive we are conscious of every gear change and every glance in the mirror. After a year of driving we may not even realize that we have just glanced up to the mirror and certainly do not ask ourselves, 'Should I change down?' each time we do. Time and practice is needed to move from one stage to the next. In the same way we cannot push children straight into 'automatic mode'. They only take responsibility because they have been given responsibility. We help them to reduce the dangers by allowing independence to develop gradually – one step at a time.

The Golden Rules of Parenting

Becoming street-wise

- Walk with them; if you want them to learn how to be pedestrians, they need to walk the streets. You cannot learn how to cross the road by sitting in the back of the car.

- Start by letting them make a trip that does not involve crossing the road (posting a letter, going around to a friend's). This is well within the grasp of most five- to six-year-olds.

- Watch as they cross the last road (but only the road is quiet or there is a crossing point), then let them finish the trip into school themselves (by the age of six or seven).

- They should be able to go to the shops, take a bus to town, walk to school and go around to a friend's house before they are eleven.

In the same way, you should gradually allow children to do the washing (help sort into light and colours, cotton and wool, read labels, put in machine and select programme), and to cook (starting with cereal at five, and ending with the family's evening meal by eleven).

77 Divided you fall: parents have to agree.

Parents have to agree. If they do not, the children will drive a wedge between them. If each parent has a different set of rules, children are confused. Ideally rules should be discussed before a child is born, but most of us do not do so. Parents usually do not realize they disagree about how to bring up children until they are already doing the job.

Our main experience of parenting comes from being parented, and unless we make a concerted effort we tend to follow in our own parents' mould. Problems arise when partners' family styles are different.

In the first months of a baby's life disagreement probably does not matter that much, but as children grow up, consistency between parents becomes more and more important. If you do not sort it out, the children learn to play one of you off against the other.

The Golden Rules of Parenting

- Remember that your partner grew up with the regime he is suggesting. Are the results really such a disaster? Could you meet each other halfway?
- Write down what is important to you. Is anything not negotiable?
- Write down what is fairly important to you. How far are you prepared to move?
- Write down what is not important.
- Negotiate. If you cannot agree, prepare your case.
- Let each person state his principles and give his reasons.
- Try to negotiate again.
- Write down what is agreed, so that if necessary you can refer back to it.

Ultimately, we have to allow that if one person does most of the caregiving, they also have the lion's share of deciding the day-to-day upbringing of the children.

78 Put yourself in their shoes.

Sometimes it pays to stand back and try to see things from a child's point of view. You may not care if someone uses your cup, but because preschool children have not yet developed a fully internalized sense of identity or a complete understanding of what it is to be 'me' rather than 'you', possessions are not just possessions to them; they are part of themselves.

- He is 'the little boy who has the red coat, the blue bike and the Thomas the Tank Engine cup'. From his point of view, it really does matter that the cup belongs to him.
- Just because he insists on doing it his way does not mean he is being awkward. It is because he lacks skills and finesse that he needs to practise. If he did not insist on trying he would never learn to be independent and self-sufficient.
- He tries it out on you because it is much safer for him to do so. You will forgive and forget; others might not.

  The Golden Rules of Parenting

- He is jealous and angry because you have a new baby. He is hurt because you are delighted. Put yourself in his shoes. If your partner moved the baby-sitter into your bed, your child might be delighted, but you would no doubt feel angry and jealous.

Stepping back to see things from another point of view gives all of us a deeper insight into the situation. Children over five are capable of putting themselves in another's shoes, and it sometimes helps to talk this through with them. Before four they are quite incapable of doing so; expecting them to is just a waste of time!

79 Say it once.

If he knows you will ask him three times, why should he do anything until you have? If you threaten twice before carrying out your threat, he gets extra time. If you threaten but never carry through, he can ignore you completely.

- Say exactly what you mean and mean exactly what you say.
- Say it once.
- Act.

If there is likely to be some delay, do not fill the space with idle threats. Just say what you want:

I want you to pick those toys up.

Ignore his prevarication and go straight to the 'one, two, three'.

I am going to count to three and if you have not started to clear up by then you will go straight to your room. One, two, three . . .

If he does what you have asked, thank him. If he does not:

Go to your room, and come down when you are ready to pick up the toys. If I have to pick them up for you, they will go on the confiscation shelf for a day.

Do not threaten more than you will carry through. You are not going to throw everything in the bin, so do not say that you will. Do not threaten to confiscate toys for a week if you know very well that he will be able to wheedle them out of you by Wednesday.

80 Actions speak louder than words: you have to walk the talk.

Adults can look and listen; they can even look, listen, look and do something else at the same time. The part of an adult's brain that controls attention has both a fully developed capacity and mature organization. Small children have neither. While adults hold about seven items in mind, toddlers hold one or two. Adults concentrate for long periods and filter out distractions because they can switch in and out with ease. They can look up, say hello and switch right back to what they were doing. Tiny children find this almost impossible; older children still find it difficult.

Unlike adults, the centre of a small child's world is focused 'out there' rather than in his mind. This means that what he sees has a much more dominating influence on how he acts and what he believes to be true. If your voice says one thing and your body another it is your actions that he takes on board.

Don't give mixed messages. A preschooler will 'do as I do not do as I say' because that is what comes most naturally.

Everyone finds it easier to follow the messages if they all sing the same tune; if the illustrations fit the story, the talk the actions. Children want the main points emphasized. They want the body language, the tone of voice and the facial expressions to all line up – which is probably why we emphasize these things so much when we talk to children.

Children learn about social relationships, social interactions and social expectations first and foremost by watching their loved ones, doing what they do. Parents and caregivers then shape these actions by approval and disapproval, reward and punishment. All future social interactions stem from this. The example parents set can make a lifetime's impression.

81 Take a good look at what you are doing.

Every once in a while, parents need to stand back and take a good and unprejudiced look at their parenting skills.

- Can my children still feel confident that I love them? As children grow up, the kisses and cuddles of the preschool years are often replaced by a less demonstrative love. By doing things together, talking, supporting and being on their side. Even though the child may initiate this more standoffish attitude, he may still find the absence of physical affection unsettling.
- Am I giving more attention to bad behaviour than I am to good behaviour?
- Am I spending more time criticizing them than praising them?
- Do I practise what I preach?
- Am I instilling confidence? Do they know I am on their side? Are my expectations realistic? Do I reward effort?

  The Golden Rules of Parenting

- Do I expect them to do the right thing? Do I reward them when they do? Do I expect them to do their best? Do they know?

- Has my parenting changed as they have grown? Am I still treating them as if they were younger? Am I letting go? Am I encouraging them to branch out from the strong base I have provided at home? Is the family moving on?

- Am I allowing enough independence? (It is always a bit more than seems comfortable.) Could they walk to school? Could they go to the shops? Could they make their own breakfast?

- Do I expect enough from them? Am I still taking ownership of problems that they should be dealing with themselves? Am I still asking if they have washed behind their ears, am I still doing their washing when they could do it for themselves?

- Do they know where they stand? Are the limits I have set clear? Have those limits changed as they have grown up and matured?

82 Don't take ownership of their problems.

If you always cope with your children's problems, they will go on creating them because there is no motivation for them to stop. Why should he remember his gym kit if he knows you will always run after him if he forgets?

The primary responsibility of the parents of babies and toddlers is to love and care for their children, to nourish them and protect from harm. As they grow up, parental responsibilities also include teaching, enabling and training children, particularly training in how to behave in socially and culturally acceptable ways.

Once children reach the 'age of reason', at about seven, our role subtly changes and we need to start handing over responsibility for their actions. It is time to ask the question 'Who owns the problem?'

The Golden Rules of Parenting

The people who own the problem are those who are affected by it, and their ownership is in direct proportion to who suffers as a consequence of inaction. So, for example, forgetting his packed lunch is his problem because it only affects the child. Only the child goes hungry when his lunch remains on the kitchen table.

If you find it difficult to sort all this out it may help you to:

- Make a list of all problems.
- Assign responsibilities for each problem.
- Consider the consequences of any action you might take.

Formal lists help us to step outside the problem and see it from a more dispassionate point of view. Once we have taken the emotion and blame out of the equation it is easier to see:

- How to make the consequences of the situation clear to all parties.
- What would be a more desirable outcome.
- How to act to bring this about.

83 Give your child choices.

Nobody likes being told exactly what to do. Sooner or later they are likely to rebel and do exactly the opposite of what is asked, just for the hell of it. Unless there is iron discipline and stiff punishments, it is difficult to keep control.

Nobody learns to take responsibilities for their actions unless they feel they can make a choice. So why not give one?

We can go to the park now, or have a story first. It's your choice.

You can wear the red T-shirt or the blue one, it's your choice. I'm sorry the Harry Potter T-shirt is not a choice today because it is in the wash. You can choose it tomorrow.

You can pick up the toys now or you can go to your room until you are ready to pick up your toys, it is your choice.

You can collect up the Lego now and put it away in the cupboard, or you can leave it for me to pick up and put on the confiscation shelf. It is your choice.

You can get dressed now or you can put your clothes in the car and get dressed outside the school gates. It is your choice.

You can eat your greens or take a vitamin tablet – it's your choice.

But remember that a choice is a choice. If they choose to get dressed in the back of the car outside the school gates, you should carry through. If they don't pick up the Lego and you confiscate it until Wednesday, don't give it back on Tuesday.

84 Expect them to be helpful – and create an environment where this comes naturally.

Small children are often spontaneously helpful and kind, because most people are spontaneously helpful and kind to them. As they grow up, they enter into a much more competitive world, in which they are expected to do their best to be the best. Being top dog is largely incompatible with being helpful and kind, and our once helpful children stop being so cooperative and start expecting someone else to pick up on the chores.

No one is going to do the dirty jobs if they can avoid it. Especially if they see that others are managing to avoid their share.

- Expect them to help. Everyone over three should have their tasks. It is part of being grown-up. Three-year-olds can put their clothes in the dirty washing basket before they get into the bath. They can get their socks from the drawer, and hold the pegs while you put the washing on the line.

- By six they should have taken over responsibility for some of the joint household tasks, such as helping clear the table and stacking the dishwasher, washing up, vacuuming their bedroom or putting out the rubbish with you.
- In addition to joint household responsibilities, children should, gradually, take over responsibility for their own welfare: picking up their things, making their bed and making their packed lunch.

It is always the case that as we make our beds, so we lie in them. If mothers begin by doing everything for their partners and families, they tend to get left with the chores. The only way to avoid this is to make a radical change. Get a chart and write up the chores and the responsibilities. A point system works quite well with, say, one point for vacuuming the lounge and three points for cooking dinner.

Obviously a certain amount of flexibility is needed here; there are times when they are too tired or have homework. Rather than stepping in yourself every time, cancel chores for the night for everyone. Nothing is set in stone. If it is not working, look at the rota again.

85 When you make changes, it gets worse before it gets better.

Change is not easy. You cannot change how children behave unless you make changes to how you behave – which means, inevitably, that there is a certain amount of stress and insecurity on all sides.

Security is strongest when everything is familiar. It is easy to go on as you are because your behaviour patterns have become automatic and no one has to think what they have to do.

When other people try to change how children act, they feel both stressed and insecure. Why don't people like them the way they were?

- Insecurity makes it likely that children will act up, and attention-seeking behaviours come to the forefront.
- Change necessarily goes against the mould. Your child becomes more stressed because the old automatic ways of doing things no longer work.
- Change takes effort.
- He has to work out what the new limits are. That means pushing up against them.

So expect it to get quite a lot worse before it gets better. But hold on in there. It will work out. Just stand firm until it does.

86 Don't draw them into your problems.

All relationships have their ups and downs, and when under stress it is more difficult to keep one's temper. The stresses and strains on families with young children are huge. If both parents work, there are organizational problems and time pressures. If one parent chooses to stay at home, there may be money difficulties and resentments.

If you are going through a difficult patch:

- Don't expect or encourage children to take sides.
- Protect their neutrality; they should be allowed to be loyal to you both.
- Do not use the children as a sounding board for complaints against your partner.
- Do not let the children overhear you complaining about your partner.
- Try not to fight in front of the children.
- Small children take things at face value; be careful what you say in front of them. They may take you literally.

  The Golden Rules of Parenting

- Do not give the impression that there are secret discussions behind the scenes. Accept that if children worry they are likely to behave badly. Try to understand, but do not accept bad behaviour.
- Explain. Do not assume children will not notice what is going on. What we know is seldom as problematic as the things we imagine.
- Sometimes we say things we later regret. If you say something that could worry the children, explain:

  I didn't mean what I said about Daddy. I was just cross and being silly. There is nothing to worry about. Daddy and I are friends again now.

Children copy what we do. If parents often quarrel and fight, so do their children. Children can also learn how to play victim or bully from watching the interactions between their parents.

TECHNIQUE

87 Put on a poker face: there are times when you must hide your feelings.

It follows that if your child is doing certain things because they gain him your undivided attention, you need to learn how to stop showing how you feel when he behaves badly. Such as not showing you are:

- Shocked when he swears at Grandma.
- Embarrassed when he masturbates in the supermarket.
- Angry when he refuses to get in his pushchair.

The easiest way to hide your feelings is to practise taking a poker stance:

- Speak in a totally flat, expressionless voice.
- Stand in a stiff, unyielding position.
- Most important of all, put on a blank, unexpressive face.
- Avert your eyes, and speak to the child, if you must, with your gaze fixed in the middle distance.

The Golden Rules of Parenting

When a small child behaves badly, adopt this stance:

- Pick him up (or pick yourself up) and without comment put physical or emotional distance between you.
- Keep up the cold poker stance for as long as he is badly behaved.
- Once he changes mood, switch back to your normal warm and welcoming self.

88 Saying sorry is not enough; there are six steps to a full apology.

Georgie, I'm sorry I lost my temper with you. Can we make up and be friends?

Sam, I'm sorry I forgot to wash your best T-shirt. I'll put it in the washer now so you can have it tomorrow.

Sorry I'm home later than I intended.

Sorry I am being selfish. I didn't mean to hurt your feelings.

It never hurts to apologize. But saying sorry is only the first step. Those who need to apologize should also:

- Admit they did wrong without lying about it first.
- Explain what they were thinking or trying to do – even if they were just being careless or thoughtless.
- Acknowledge the hurt and harm they have caused.
- Affirm that they wish to regain the friendship and respect of those they hurt.
- Make amends if possible; if not, offer something – a gift, a helping hand – to show you want to repay them for the harm caused.
- Learn by mistakes. Think about (and with a small child talk about) how things can be done differently in future.

Remember that these six steps apply to all the family. If you wrong a child, you need to take these steps for them, just as they need to take them for you or their siblings if they do wrong.

89 Don't rush in – it may be exactly what he wants you to do.

He deliberately pushes his dinner off his plate. You say, 'No!' and he immediately does it again.

'Me do it!' he shouts, struggling with his sock and glaring at you, almost daring you to intervene. You can see that the heel is going to end up on top of his foot and that in his present mood that means he is going to scream with fury. But what do you gain by wading in? He will have that tantrum anyway – because he wants to do it himself and get it right (an impossibility as things stand).

Sometimes the best way to deal with it is to walk away and let him get on with it.

- Children don't have tantrums if we are not around.
- They don't play silly games for our attention if we are not there to see.
- All you do by intervening is up the stakes and teach the child that this is a pretty good way to get Mummy on his case.
- If it's safe to walk away, just walk away.

  The Golden Rules of Parenting

Sometimes distraction works in these situations. Instead of playing his game and letting him mess about with his food, get him to play yours.

So you've finished have you? Let's wipe your hands and you can go off and play.

Whoops, look at the time, we'll have to gobble down our breakfast if we are going to get to the park this morning.

You can leave those socks till we are ready to go out if you want to, I need you to clean the sink in your own special way.

90 If you wait for him to make the first move, you wait for ever. Remember, your child won't change unless and until you do.

We tend to think of our own child's bad behaviour as the child's fault, although we are usually ready to accept that the bad behaviour of other people's children is, at least in part, the result of how the parents have dealt with that child's behaviour in the past.

In fact, the behaviour of all children is the result of an interaction between caregiver and child. Some children are naturally easygoing, and parenting them is relatively easy. Others have more difficult temperaments and this makes it much harder for them to stay in control.

Some children find it hard to keep negative emotions under control, to concentrate or pay attention, and where this is the case, it is very much harder for caregivers to ignore a child's disruptive and difficult behaviour. It is all very well to say that we should give more attention to good behaviour, but if the quiet times when the children are being good and amusing

  The Golden Rules of Parenting

themselves rarely happen, the temptation to read the paper, or make a phone call (thus moving your attention elsewhere) is overwhelming. The best tactic here, is to look up and smile at them as you read and make the occasional comment from the phone, so it is clear to the children that even when you are doing your own thing, you are still emotionally engaged.

The important point to remember is that however a child's behavioural problems arose, strategies that are not working now are most unlikely to start working next month. Children will not change their behaviour of their own accord.

Which means that if we want them to change, we have to make the first move. We have to change.

91 Sometimes you need to make a special effort to break the cycle.

A familiar pattern puts both sides in readiness for the usual battle. Habits persist unless a real effort is made to change. Anticipatory learning (Pavlovian conditioning) forms a deep rut which makes travelling the habitual course effortless. We are drawn down our old familiar furrow because it's so much easier than taking a new route.

To change, you have to break out of the furrow, to alter things so that A does not invariably lead to B. Which is hard, if not impossible, for a child to initiate. Parents are motivated to change because they can think ahead and see the benefits. Small children cannot.

- Parents must initiate change.
- Once we stop responding to a child's behaviour in the normal way, the furrow is cracked.
- His behaviour is now more amenable to change.

Instead of getting upset about the toys all over the floor, do something about it.

- Explain.
  Any toys which are not picked up will be confiscated.

- Warn.
  Confiscation zone coming up in three minutes.

- Act.
  I have confiscated the toys left on the floor until tomorrow.

Make sure you mean it.

92 Sometimes you have to get really tough.

Parenting is not just about allowing the delicate unfolding of a child's individuality. It is also about raising him to fit into the larger social world. Which means that a child must know how to behave in a way that is appropriate. However tolerant we are about certain aspects of his behaviour, we can be pretty sure that other people will be less so.

We do a child a disservice if we do not make clear to him those rules that make his behaviour acceptable to the outside world.

Jamie, there are rules about bottoms and willies and you are old enough to know them. Now you're a big boy, do not let other people see your bottom except on the beach or in the bath. You can play with your willy in your bedroom, but not when other people can see you. That is the rule.

Some things are absolute.

We do not swear in this house, swearing is unacceptable.

I will not accept rudeness. I expect you to apologize.

Hitting is not allowed. Go to your rooms until you have calmed down and can behave in an acceptable manner.

Other things are relative.

William, I know we sometimes swear, but Grandma does not. Remember, it is Grandma's home and she can decide what people do when they visit. We have to abide by her rules when we are in her house.

Be firm, be consistent, make the message clear – and let the child know the sanctions.

That's the rule and you have broken it. Go to your room for five minutes.

That's the rule. I warned you that if you broke it again you would not be able to play on your computer tonight. I am taking away the lead, I will give it back in the morning.

Make sure the punishment fits the crime – and never threaten what you will not carry out.

Technique 203

93 Whatever you read or hear, children can survive without a varied diet.

Children who are starving are unhappy and lethargic. If a child is boisterous and happy, he is not deprived of food. Trace elements are vital for our health; if we are deprived of them we become ill. It follows that a healthy child is not deprived of trace elements.

If he is healthy, active and happy, he has the food he needs.

While other small animals have milk teeth the main ingredient of their diet is milk. So, for example, baby chimps are weaned at about three to four years and lose their milk teeth at four. By analogy, milk should play a major role in the diet of children with milk teeth. Because milk contains most of the trace elements we need (the match isn't perfect because cow's milk is designed for baby cows, not human children), a child who is getting plenty of milk is getting what he needs.

A diet of milk, potatoes, some carrots and a green vegetable such as broccoli or peas is excellent. It does not need to change every day. Once children start school we reduce the dependence on milk (some children are intolerant of lactose in later

  The Golden Rules of Parenting

childhood) and move towards the recommended daily helpings of fruit and vegetables, carbohydrates, fats and proteins. But even then a child does not need variety. If you have found a few meals that he likes and he is thriving – stick with it and introduce new foods occasionally to see how he reacts.

Variety may be the spice of life, but like spice it is not an essential. For hundreds of years the basic diet of most Europeans was a staple (bread, pasta, potatoes, dumplings), seasonal or dried fruit and vegetables (and this could mean cabbage every day of the week), occasional eggs, milk and a little meat or cheese. If they hadn't survived on it, we would not be here.

It is great if he does, but don't fret if your child doesn't eat his greens!

Because toxins and food attacked by bacteria taste bitter or sour, children have a built-in mechanism that makes them reject bitter and sour tastes. Which is why many children hate sprouts! The sensitivity drops as we grow up (and being violently sick is less likely to kill us), and can be overcome if we regularly eat bitter foods. It is activated again in the first months of pregnancy – which, because of the dangers of toxins to the developing foetus, is a very sensible state of affairs.

94 There is a built-in mechanism that stops children eating strange foods. You activate it at your peril.

All animals have a built-in mechanism that makes them wary of eating strange foods. Humans are no exception. Faced with a new food, we try a tiny amount, wait to see if it makes us ill, and if it doesn't, we try a little more. It's how we avoid being poisoned.

The wide variety of food we now eat has reduced the influence of this mechanism for most adults, but it is still very active in children. In some children it is particularly sensitive. If your child is one of those who have a sensitive mechanism, it will always be difficult to introduce new foods. If you try to fight the mechanism, you will make things worse. Just as we struggle for breath when our airways are blocked, a child's 'poison detector' will fight to reject food if we try to force it on him.

The way to introduce new foods to such children is:

- Mix extremely tiny amounts into a well-loved and familiar 'carrier' food (such as milk, rice or potato).
- Once the child has accepted half a teaspoonful mixed into potato (and I really do mean half a teaspoon), increase the proportion of the new food very, very gradually until the child is taking a 50/50 mix.
- Now reduce the carrier very gradually until the child is taking the new food 'neat'.
- The stronger the flavour, the smaller the steps.
- Be patient: it could take weeks.

So, for example we might wean babies on to potato with milk. Once the child is happy, add the tiniest amount of lentil. Gradually increase this and reduce the potato. Instead of lentil we could use carrot, peas and cheese so that we have four foods the child finds acceptable. A base of milk and rice can be used to introduce fruit in the same way. For sensitive children we will need to use this procedure whenever we introduce a new food.

95 You can win the mealtime battles.

Giving children a varied and well-balanced diet is a media obsession that is hard to resist. We read that too much fat causes obesity, with the inevitable problems of heart disease, cancer, high blood pressure and strokes. Too little fibre, fruit and vegetables and we have strokes, and bowel problems. E numbers and additives cause behavioural problems and cancer. Not to mention sweets, the wrong sort of fats, and processed foods.

Yet in spite of all these horrors we are living longer. In the nineteenth century life expectancy was about fifty, now it's closing in on eighty. All the time children are getting brighter and healthier. If an average child took an IQ test designed for children in 1910, he would almost certainly come out in the 'exceptional' range. We no longer eat food which has been contaminated by rats or washed in water containing harmful bacteria, and those who serve our food now wash their hands before serving us and are careful about cross-infections.

In other words, we should take the dire warnings about the horrors that result from a modern diet with a pinch of salt. Most of

  The Golden Rules of Parenting

what is said is true (or partly so), but the effects are small and have to be balanced against the stress caused by imposing a particular diet on a child against the child's wishes. There is no doubt at all that stress is bad for health, behaviour and happiness and makes people vulnerable to illness, heart disease and depression.

- Throw out your obsessions together with the snack foods. Make mealtimes relaxed.
- Make changes – if you can eat in a different place, do; if not, get a new tablecloth or change your child's place.
- Choose something he will eat. Put it in front of him, let him eat what he wants. Accept that children do not like bitter tastes.
- Then let him go and play. Do not comment on what he leaves on his plate.
- Children do not need variety. If he'll eat potatoes he does not need pasta. If he'll eat chicken he does not need lamb. If in doubt give him a glass of milk and a vitamin pill.
- Accept that a healthy, active and happy child is well fed.
- Don't give food between meals.
- After a week or so, set new ground rules. He selects what he wants to eat and agrees to eat what is on his plate.

96 The best way to deal with tantrums is to ignore them.

Somewhere between sixty and eighty per cent of all two- to three-year-old children have tantrums – and most have them every day. It's a normal and natural part of growing up. Tantrums can be frustrating, embarrassing or alarming. Children become difficult, refusing to be strapped in car seats, demanding sweets, refusing to walk or hold hands. They throw things, they hit out, they may even bite their arm until it bleeds or bang their head on the floor until they raise a lump.

But however much we are upset by such behaviour there is little doubt that the person who is hurt most is the child. Yet as many parents will confirm, it sometimes seems as if the child deliberately goes out of his way to have a tantrum, demanding things that he knows full well cannot be given, like sitting on the driver's lap while he drives, or refusing help with buttons he cannot manage to fasten.

The basic way of dealing with tantrums is:

- Put on a poker stance, remove all expression from your face, your voice and your body.
- Either walk away (if it is safe and convenient to do so), or pick up the child and put him outside the room (if it is less disruptive to you, and to the rest of the family, to remove him).
- Pick him up and hold him very tight. Either look directly into his eyes without any expression, or, if you find it easier, avert your eyes so it is clear you are not looking at him. Hold tight until he stops the tantrum.
- Then, whichever method you have used, cuddle (if he wants to), talk about it (if he needs to) and forgive and forget.

Younger children generally spring back to normality very quickly; older children may remain sad and sorry and in need of comfort. Play it by ear.

97 Start as you mean to go on: establish bedtime rules for babies by the end of the first week.

The sooner you establish the difference between a baby's day sleeps (sleeping in his pram or on the sofa, in the light) and his night sleeps (in his cot, curtains drawn, no distractions), the better.

- Set up a night sleeping space without toys (toys are for play spaces not sleeping spaces). Night sleeps should be in a dark room. (This is important for the proper development of his eyes.)
- Establish a nightly routine. Give him a bath, change him into his nightclothes, draw the bedroom curtains, turn down the light and feed him, using the place and position you will use for night feeds.
- After the feed (whether or not he is asleep), put him into his cot, turn off the light, say goodnight and leave.
- Ignore mild protests, now and throughout the night. He must learn to go back to sleep.
- It may help a fretful child if you rub your hands and face on

  The Golden Rules of Parenting

his sheet (the sweat glands in your hands and face are oily and give off your characteristic smell).

- Everyone wakes in the night. It is vital that he is not distracted from falling off to sleep again should this happen.
- While he still needs a night feed, keep the cot beside the bed so you do not have to get up. If using formula put measured water in one bottle and measured formula in another; combine the two when he wakes. It is not necessary to warm night feeds. Lift, feed and return to the cot. Do not change him unless absolutely necessary.

The daytime pattern should be different.
- He should sleep in a different room from his night sleeps.
- Let him fall asleep after a feed; put him in his pram or on the sofa. If he needs encouragement, rock him until he falls asleep. Bear in mind that you are teaching him to take a cat-nap when and wherever he needs one. A consistent daytime pattern is not a great help in learning this.
- It will make it easier for him to distinguish cat-naps from night sleeps if you leave the lights on during the day and do not try to impose complete silence or remove distractions.

98 If you got it wrong to begin with, you can re-establish night-time sleep rules. But it's tough going.

1 Stop using the cot for daytime sleeps.

2 Prepare the room. All toys should be out of sight in a box or cupboard. No mobiles or musical boxes. Rub your hands and face on a teddy so it smells of you, then tuck it in with him.

3 Get him used to sleeping in the dark. If he is used to a night-light or to light from the street, gradually reduce the level of light in the room. Find some light-proof linings for your curtains. Stay with him while he gets used to being in the dark.

4 Prepare the child. Stop singing or stroking him and just sit with him in silence until he falls asleep.

5 Remember that not sleeping at night is no problem for him. It's your lack of sleep that's the problem (refer back to rule 97 for further help).

6 You are now ready for the difficult bit. Find a time when you are free of stress and not about to go on holiday. Letting a baby cry is traumatic and seeing it through is very hard.

  The Golden Rules of Parenting

7 After feeding him put him in his cot, say goodnight, turn off the light and leave. No songs or whispers, no strokes or rocking. Just a quick and matter-of-fact goodnight. Do not look back, close the door and go downstairs.

8 He will protest – and you must let him. Stay tough, and after about four to six nights he should be putting himself to sleep. Reinforce this by setting up a consistent bedtime routine.

9 If you give in to him you simply restart the clock. It's tough. Repeat point 7 the next night, and the next, and the next. The protests will gradually get shorter until they disappear. Most parents find their child will learn to put himself to sleep within a week.

And if you cannot see it through? Again, it is your sleeplessness that is the problem here, not your baby's. He will catch up with whatever sleep he needs. So carry out the first six steps and buy the largest bed you can fit into your room. Put him to bed in his cot (or your bed) with a minimum of fuss. If he wakes in the night, put him in bed beside you and go back to sleep.

99 You need bedtime routines for older children.

1 Make a list of everything that needs to be done before bedtime. Bath, teeth, getting into pyjamas, getting tomorrow's clothes and school bags ready, remembering anything extra that needs to be taken into school (violin, gym kit, dinner money, homework books). Add all the bedtime routines (picking up toys, putting things away, reading a story, having a hot drink, a cuddle, or a song) to the list. Now add anything they may call for (a glass of water by their bed, time to find teddy). Finally add a five-minute warning time, then estimate how long this all takes (the list time).

2 Now decide on the actual tucked-up bedtime you are aiming for. This is not the time you tell them to get to bed (which is the official bedtime) but the time you want to start your child-free time. For the sake of argument, let's say this is 9 p.m.

3 Decide how long it takes to get through the list and adjust the official bedtime (the time you warn them it is bedtime in five minutes) to reach your child-free goal on time. So, for example, if the list takes an hour you need to give the warning at eight to be child-free by nine.

4   At eight, announce that it is five minutes to bedtime. Get them to pick up the toys, and finish up their games while you run their bath. When they are in their pyjamas, let them check their lists (read out the list for the younger children). The more quickly they get through the list, the longer they have for their story. But when tucked-up time comes around, it is time for lights off. No arguments, no getting out of bed, no calling out for you except in an emergency. Ignore them if they call.

5   If they keep getting up or calling out, get a comfy chair, put it outside their bedroom door and sit on watch with a good book. If they call out, ignore them. If they get up, put on a poker face and quickly and firmly put them to bed. It will take time but it works in the end. Reward them for staying in bed.

6   As children grow up, they should be allowed to read in bed.

7   Night waking is common. If a child is in a dark room (and has been trained since babyhood to go back to sleep), he will usually do so. Reinforce this by ignoring shouts and by taking him back to bed if he comes into your room too early in the morning. If he needs the toilet, take him quickly without putting on the lights and see him back to bed.

100 If you don't want them to play on the computer all day, watch TV nonstop, use the internet for hours or run up huge phone bills, make rules.

Anyone can make a rule, but there is no point whatsoever in making a rule that you do not stick to, or impose only when the mood takes you. Saying one thing and doing another simply undermines your authority.

- Engage your brain before your mouth. Be realistic. Only make rules if they concern you (how tidy your child's room is is your concern if you clean it, pick up his washing or look for things he has lost. So don't). Don't make rules you cannot police – like coming straight home from school if no one is in when he gets home.
- Stick to a rule once you have made it. If it's obvious you cannot enforce the rule, it is better to renegotiate than allow the rule to be flouted.

  The Golden Rules of Parenting

- It's wise to negotiate issues directly. Meet, let everyone have their say, then make agreements about potentially contentious issues: staying out, the phone, TV, computer, tidiness, chores, homework, returning plates, mugs and towels to their rightful place.

- Draw up agreed contracts, write everything down so you all understand what has been agreed. Sign them. Contracts should make clear which privileges are offered in exchange for compliance. For example he gets to use the internet for up to one hour every night providing he comes straight home from school and calls you if he is going to be late. That way the penalty is clear. Home late means he has chosen not to use the computer tonight. Stand firm.

- Alternatively, you can decide what happens if a rule is broken. Be realistic about the consequences. You must do as you say, so don't make the punishment one you will relent on halfway through.

- Discuss the broader issues: his safety, how much of the family budget can be given over to his needs. Talk about the need to consider other people's worries, beliefs and standards – and how much this should be taken into account.

101 The phone rules.

There are two issues here: hogging the line, and driving up the bills. Both need to be addressed.

Hogging the line

The ideal solution is a separate line for the children. Failing that, make an agreement:

- They will stay off the line, or answer briefly if you are expecting a call, especially when other children may need to call home.
- Get call interrupt, teach them to use it and ensure they let you know if there are any calls for you when they are on the line.
- Set a realistic maximum length for calls. If children can't meet their friends on the street, this is where they chat. Bear this in mind.

Costs

- Show children the family budget, and discuss with them how much of this can be spared for phone calls. Go through the bill. What is being spent on their calls? Is this reasonable? Set a limit.

- Make it clear that certain high-rate calls are off limits – and that they should not use the phone to dial long distance or to call a mobile phone, without consulting you first.

- Agree how they earn money to pay off any overspending, and at what rate overspends are deducted from pocket money.

Mobiles

- Pay as you go is the only way. It costs more but provides a natural limit – and protects you if the phone is stolen.

102 The pocket money rules.

Pocket money is not a child's by right – it is his by your indulgence, a point that you should bear in mind, and older children should be reminded of, especially if they are constantly pestering for more.

One of the main reasons for giving pocket money is to teach money management. So encourage a child to budget by saving some money towards his holidays or buying bigger items. The following points need to be taken into account.

- How much pocket money you can afford to give.
- The going rate amongst his friends. Not what he says other children get, but what their parents say they get.
- What is included in his pocket money. Does he have to use it for bus fares, subs and his mobile phone?
- Whether or not you give all the money in cash, or put some into a savings account towards his holiday spending. Does he have free access to this or does he have to discuss it with you first? Are you willing to add a bonus if he manages to save a certain amount?

The Golden Rules of Parenting

- How much of his pocket money (if any) is unconditional, and what conditions you should impose.
- Does he have to pay for deliberate breakage from his pocket money? What about damage caused by his carelessness?
- He should be free to spend the unconditional element as he wants, PROVIDING his purchases fit with family rules.
- Whether or not the child can earn additional money by helping around the house, cleaning the car and so on. (Note that some housework should be expected from all children. This is payment over and above the basic requirement.)

Examine your yearly budget, and in the light of this decide how much money you can afford to spend (or wish to spend) on each child. This should include what you spend at Christmas, for birthdays and holidays, fares, subs and club fees and pocket money. Divide this by twelve for the maximum monthly rate. If you cannot afford the going rate for pocket money AND lavish Christmas presents, something has to give. Show your child your calculations and ask him what he would prefer – more pocket money and fewer presents, or vice versa. Once an agreement is made, stick to it. Don't buy his phone card because he has spent everything on sweets. Let him learn to manage his budget.

103 And lastly ... expect the best. No one can guarantee success, but everyone can try to do the best they possibly can.

Expect your children to respect other people's:
- Property, rights, safety and opinions.

Expect them to show self-respect.
- Not to sell themselves short, in what they do or say.
- Not to sell themselves short in what they expect of themselves and the opinion they hold of themselves.
- And to accept that we all make mistakes, to admit those mistakes and to try not to let them undermine self-esteem.

Expect them to behave well.
- And they'll try hard to be good, strong, principled, helpful and kind.
- Because they will value and respect themselves, their family and friends.
- Because they will respect the rights of others.

No one succeeds all the time. But everyone can do their very best. Good luck.